# The Moving Book

# The
# MOVING
## Book

## How NOT to Panic
## at the Thought

IRENE CUMMING KLEEBERG

**Butterick Publishing**

Copyright © 1978 by Butterick Publishing, 708 Third Avenue, New York, New York 10017, a division of American Can Company.

Manufactured and printed in the United States of America. Published simultaneously in the USA and Canada.

Illustrator: Phoebe Gaughan
Book Designer: Sheila Lynch

**Library of Congress Cataloging in Publication Data**

Kleeberg, Irene Cumming.
  The moving book.

  Includes index.
  1. Moving, Household.  I.  Title.
TX307.K58     643      78-58761
ISBN 0-88421-078-2

# CONTENTS

2034437

# INTRODUCTION

Moving! The very thought of moving, or even the word *moving*, tends to make many people either laugh or shudder. Moving for most people and most families is a big job, involving not only the physical effort of weeding things out and packing them up but the emotional effort of leaving one home and moving to another.

But moving really needn't be an ordeal—or not as much of one as it sometimes seems. Moving can be organized and planned so that it will bring very few surprises with it and will prove a very satisfactory experience.

## Using This Book

This book has been divided into chapters designed to give you as much information as possible to help make your move, whether it is around the corner or almost around the world, as easy and satisfactory as possible. Charts throughout make it easy for you to review the main points that are discussed more fully in the chapters.

The beginning chapters discuss the various ways in which you can move from several points of view,

including economy and convenience. A move, like anything else, works better if it is organized. "Organizing a
Move" covers how to organize your move for maximum
efficiency.

"Starting to Pack" includes how to pack, and specific
instructions are given for those items that need special
care before they are moved. Other items can go into
boxes that you can get free from local merchants—if
you know which sizes you want. Picking up used boxes
in this way can prove a tremendous saving, as anyone
who has purchased boxes knows. And we suggest you
avoid getting boxes from the moving companies, as
these are usually over-priced.

Contrary to one school of thought, most children do
not find moving easy. Home is so important to children
that they often feel bewildered by the knowledge of an
impending move. "Helping the Kids Make the Move"
offers suggestions for making it as easy as possible for
young people.

Many people who are moving take an inventory as
part of the move so they can have a permanent record of
just what the family owns. "Taking and Making an
Inventory" discusses various ways of making one and
goes into the question of whether or not you need your
own inventory at all. To what extent, if you are using
professional movers, should you rely on their inventory?

Moving your household goods is only one part of a
move—you also have to move yourself and your family.
And since you will probably also be moving a lot of
things that were "left over," conditions may be a little
cramped. "Moving Yourself and Your Family" not only
goes into how to plan for as much comfort as possible,
but also discusses ways of moving yourself and your
family and choosing places to stay overnight.

"Working with the Movers" discusses the various

things the movers will expect of you—and what you can expect from the movers. An extremely important section deals with claims against the movers—and how to act if you do not get satisfaction on these claims.

Most people today own either plants or pets and often both, and want to take them with them when they move. It should be a fairly simple matter, but often isn't because of various regulations about moving plants or pets from one state to another. "Moving Plants and Pets" gives you information on transporting both and includes a listing of those plants that are specifically excluded from certain states.

Moving isn't over once your household goods are in your new home. You still have to become acquainted with your new community so that you feel as close to it as you did to your old one. "After You Get There— What?" discusses how to unpack and get settled in the easiest way, and how to get to know other people in the community.

The post office will forward mail to you for one year after you move—and then it's returned to the sender. You can avoid mix-ups on your mail by notifying all those people and organizations that send you mail that you've moved.

"Letting People Know" discusses various means of telling people you've moved or will be moving, and includes a listing of "don't forget" individuals and organizations so that you can be certain everyone is told who should be told.

Moving out of the continental United States, whether to Alaska or Hawaii or to a foreign country, has many things in common with moving within the United States. However, there are enough differences for there to be the possibility of unexpected problems. "Moving Out of the Continental United States" discusses some of the situations that can arise and, where the rules and regulations vary from one place to another, tells how you can get the needed information. In addition, the chapter covers moving back into the United States if you have been living in a foreign country.

If you qualify, certain of your moving expenses will be deductible from your income for tax purposes. The final chapter "The Financial Side," discusses how to determine whether or not you qualify and includes a chart listing records to keep during a move for Internal Revenue purposes. In addition, the chapter attempts to give you some idea of what a long distance move is likely to cost. While the figures given are probably high, it was felt that high figures would prove more satisfactory to more people than low ones.

The final section of the book is a brief glossary of moving terminology. An index completes the book.

In compiling this book we have been very much aware that the world of moving is one that is subject to many changes in the rules and regulations that govern most aspects of it. Airlines change their size requirements for packages that can travel with you, the Interstate Commerce Commission changes portions of the tariff regulating the professional movers, and the Internal Revenue law is changed as it concerns moves. For this reason, we have concentrated in this book on giving you information that will be true no matter how rules and regulations may be changed. In those cases where we have mentioned specific points, we have also given you the information you would need to double check.

Moving can be among the best experiences of life once you are settled in your new home. It can bring new experiences, new friends, a new way of life that can prove broadening for everyone involved. We wish you all the best with your next move.

# 1

# GETTING READY TO MOVE

Anything is easier if it is carefully planned, and this is especially true of moving. The many elements that go into most moves—combinations of distance, time, money, and, of course, human actions of one kind and another—mean that there can be no absolute program for everyone. This book, we hope, will help you organize things.

A truly organized move is more likely to prove to be an ideal than a practical reality, so start by intending to stick to a schedule, but be prepared to bend to circumstances. People move on different time schedules. For that reason we are not saying "do this six weeks before" and "do that four weeks before" when discussing the early stages of your move.

## First Things First

Once you know you're moving, find out everything you can about your new city if you are moving to an unfamiliar one. Get as much advice and information about the city as you can from friends living there, real estate agents, and reading. The Chamber of Commerce or the tourist bureau or both can often be very helpful.

This is the time, too, to decide in what type of community you want to live and the type of home you hope to find. If you've always lived in cities, you may want to try living in the suburbs; if you've always lived in apartments, a house might be appealing. On the other hand, you may want to stay with what you know. In any case, you should give some thought to these questions early. There will probably be some trading off before you find your new home. The questions below may help you narrow things down.

## The Schools

Are good schools important to you? Even if you have no children, good schools should be important. If you have school-age children, of course, the question of school quality is very important.

How do you find out if the schools are good? If you ask most people in a neighborhood or most real estate agents, "Are the schools good?" they will answer "Yes," and why shouldn't they? Most public schools in the United States probably are good, their level of goodness determined largely by how much the parents and other adults in the community care about them.

However, some schools may be very much into educational experimentation, and other schools may be very rigid. Some schools may be all right but not really good, because taxes and therefore teacher salaries are so low that the best teachers are attracted to other communities with higher pay. Some schools may have open classrooms and be very proud of their open classroom program. You may think your children do better in a more structured environment. On the other hand, you may find the local schools are very traditional in approach and you would prefer a more open approach. If you do have strong opinions, it's better to know what the schools are like in advance than later on.

How can you find out more about the schools? One good way—this applies to neighborhood information in general, too—is through a friend or acquaintance. You can also ask your real estate agent, but don't rely solely on other people if you can help it.

The best way to find out about schools is to visit them. Since most communities are anxious to have the schools make a good impression and act as a selling point to prospective residents, most communities won't give you any trouble about visiting if you go about it the right way. The right way, generally speaking, is to go to the superintendent's office (rather than the school) first and have that office help you arrange to visit. You can do this on the telephone.

Can you really learn much from visiting a school? Yes, a surprising amount. In addition to the physical plan you'll get an idea of the general attitude in the school and the general educational and disciplinary cast of mind.

If you visit, for instance, the third grade your child will enter, you'll be able to tell by sitting in the classroom for a while whether the academic work is at about the same level as in the school your child is leaving.

At the same time, in walking through the halls, you'll be able to tell by the noise level—a hum, of course, is preferable to an uproar—something about the discipline in the school.

If you can't bear what you see, consider another neighborhood, visit some other schools, think about a non-public school (if such exist in the area), or plan to change your mind and make the best of it.

## The Neighborhood

Do you want a neighborhood with a strong neighborhood feeling, or do you want one where people are fairly reserved?

In theory, cities breed aloofness, while the country and suburbs are friendlier. In practice, some city neighborhoods will kill you with kindness (these are often ones with active block or neighborhood associations) and some suburb and country neighborhoods will chill you to the very bone with their aloofness.

How can you tell? A good real estate agent will often have the feel of different neighborhoods down pat and can steer you correctly. If you have a friend or an acquaintance who lives where you are about to move, that person can give you lots of information, although amateurs, as opposed to the professional agent, tend to see their own neighborhoods as the only possible ones and all others as much less desirable.

Whether friendly or cool, are the neighbors your kind of people? Lots of people have fallen in love with a neighborhood because of the way the houses look only to discover after moving in that they can't stand the neighbors who are all Republicans or Democrats or keepers of elephants.

Living in a neighborhood with people who are different from you in one way or another may be just what you want. You may find "different" people stimulating and interesting. On the other hand, you may feel that it can be pretty lonely living in a neighborhood where you can't express a political opinion without having an argument. If you feel that way, find out ahead of time what neighborhoods have people who are likely to agree with you.

How do you find out? Again, real estate agents can be good at telling you this kind of thing, although they won't help you to be a bigot. Election results will tell you something, although they may vary from year to year. The political party you prefer should be able to give you some information.

Do you want to be extremely private, so that you can't see another house from your house? Then you should not only be sure that one can't be seen now, but (if you plan to stay a long time) you had better also be sure that development isn't planned near you or within your view.

*Being able to walk to the grocery store and other shops is one advantage of living close to the center of town.*

In choosing a neighborhood, try to take careful inventory of the things that are important to you. Do you want to be able to walk to the center of town to shop or exchange your library books? If so, there's no point in buying a house miles from a town center.

Will your children be able to walk to school, or will they have to take a bus—either a school bus or a public bus? If this matters to you, be sure to find your house either where they can walk, along an established school bus route, or near a public bus.

Most people don't seem to mind (much) driving to shops for groceries, but you may prefer to walk, either because you don't have a car or because you want the

When you are selecting a neighborhood find out the distance from the house to the school.

exercise. If that's the case, make sure that the little grocery store around the corner from your new home that seems so convenient isn't really a very expensive delicatessen.

Are there special ethnic foods that are the basis of your diet? If you have a choice of neighborhoods, and one or two have the foods you like, it's worth trying a little harder to find a place you like in such an area.

## What Will It Cost?

Of course, where we live is often subject to other considerations than where we'd like to live. Whether you buy or rent, the price of the house or apartment or whatever will be the first problem. Folk wisdom, by the way, says that the price of a house or apartment is always more than you think it should be.

If you're buying, the price you can pay, and therefore the size of the house you can buy, will also be determined by the type of mortgage you can get, unless you plan to pay cash, which very few people do. Shop around for a mortgage, going from one financial institution to another to get the best deal.

Mortgage rates are controlled by the states, which means that on occasion you can get a much better deal on a mortgage by going across the border for your money than by staying in-state. It's nice, and tactful, to patronize local banks, but if you can get a better arrangement elsewhere, give it serious consideration.

## Apartment or House

We mentioned earlier apartments versus houses. Any move will take you to a different type of home, but a move from an apartment to a house or a house to an apartment can be a real shock.

Do you want a house or an apartment? If you're moving to an area that's unfamiliar to you, keep in mind that you may not always have a true choice on this. Some parts of the country have few houses, or few apartments, so although you might prefer the one or the other, you may have to forget your preference. The choice may not exist, but if it does, don't jump to the idea that you would love one or the other unless you have had experience with it. People who move to houses from apartments often mention the problems they have in getting used to them, including running up and down the stairs (if any), hearing funny noises as the heat moves down to its night setting, and feeling somewhat vulnerable at every passing noise from outside.

Furthermore, people who move to houses, even if the house is a rented one, usually find living in a house brings more do-it-yourself responsibility than ever dreamt of in an apartment. Storm windows and screens usually have to be put up and taken down. Snow, if any, has to be shoveled. Yards have to be planned, planted, mowed, trimmed, raked.

Most repairs are your responsibility, and most people living in houses find they quickly become surprisingly skillful at a lot of things they never thought they'd need to know how to do.

The person or family who moves from an apartment to a house has one type of experience. The person or family moving to an apartment from a house has another—a lot of it to do with space.

Although some apartments or apartment buildings make provision for tenant storage, most don't. You'll find yourself without an attic or cellar or breezeway or garage or wherever it was you stored the many things any home needs, from bicycles to ladders.

Partly because of this lack of storage space, most apartments seem smaller than most houses, even if they actually measure about the same. Furniture that seemed a normal size in a house may overwhelm an apartment—or you may find you can't get it in the door at all.

Before you move that grand piano, for instance, you should be sure it will fit in the door of your apartment and onto the elevator or up the stairs or, alternatively, that you can arrange to have it brought up the side of the building and in through the window—a highly

*Before you move that grand piano make sure it will fit through the doorway!*

entertaining proceeding but usually an extremely expensive one.

In all moving it's a good idea to weed out as much stuff as you possibly can. This goes double when you're moving from a house to an apartment or a smaller house, and triple if you're moving into a mobile home, which is usually already furnished.

## Selling Your Home

If you own a house or an apartment already, you'll probably want to sell it before you take possession of your new home.

Should you list it with a real estate agent, with many real estate agents, or try to sell it yourself? There are lots of opinions, and since the real estate market is fairly volatile the opinions people have often depend on how hard or easy it was to sell their house or apartment.

In favor of using an agent is the fact that you'll save your own time. The agent can help you set a realistic asking price for the house or apartment and, after all, people who are looking to buy are very likely to go to a real estate agent. A conscientious agent can also advise you on things to do to make the house more salable (fix the fence, for instance) although this may not always happen.

One real estate agent with an "exclusive listing" may work harder at selling your home than many. Listing your house or apartment with many real estate agents is usually called "multiple listing." It means that any one of a group of agents can show and sell your house. In theory, it sounds terrific, but some people who have tried multiple listing felt the agents neglected their houses in order to work on selling the exclusives.

It's possible to sell your house yourself, but it's not usually recommended. You save the agent's commission (usually at least six percent of the total selling price), but this may not make up for the disadvantages.

The problems with selling the house yourself include the emotional ones. It's very difficult seeing people go through your home coldly and mutter things like, "Well, the first thing I'd do is to rip down that terrible paper in the bathroom!"

Secondly, it takes time to show people through your house, time to answer their telephone calls, time to wait for them (and sometimes have them not show up at all) when there are lots of things you should be doing or could be doing away from the house.

If you do decide to sell the house yourself, make sure you have an outsider give you a reasonable estimate of what it should sell for at the time you're selling it. You can try a real estate broker (there would be a fee) but brokers aren't always willing to appraise houses they won't be selling. If you have no luck with a real estate broker, you can find a professional appraiser who, also for a fee, will help you arrive at a realistic estimate of your home's worth.

In any case, even though you are planning to sell your home, it is important to fix it up if you have any time at all. Even little things help. One woman mowed the lawn and raked the gravel driveway and got $2,000 more from the people the house was sold to than they had originally offered. Reason? "We hadn't realized the house looked so nice." They didn't know what influenced their decision, but she did.

## FIXING UP YOUR HOME

How do you fix up your home? The following will give you some ideas. Obviously, if you're selling an apartment, you'll be concerned with less than if you're selling a house. In any case, try the following—or some of them—and don't worry if you can't do everything.

- Mow the grass; trim the edges.
- Trim the hedges and shrubs.
- Hide or take to the dump (or whatever the practice is in your present community) baskets of leaves or weeds.
- Paint. You probably won't paint the whole house, but do paint the trim. If you can't paint all the trim on the outside, at least paint the front door—perhaps in a bright color.
- Clean the gutters. If a prospective owner is the inquiring kind, gutters full of leaves are a sure turnoff.
- If there's a pool or pond of any size filled with water, be sure you aren't breeding algae in it and if you are, clear it out.
- If there's a barbecue grill, clean out all the old leaves and dead ashes so it looks ready for dinner.
- Make sure the rooms inside are neat, much neater than they would be ordinarily. The prospective buyer is trying to figure out how large they are, and neatness helps them look larger.
- The bathrooms and kitchen should be spotless and, since kitchen cupboards are a big concern, the things inside should be neat as a pin.
- Freshly painted or freshly washed woodwork will help sell your home.
- Wash the windows—people like light houses—and open the blinds, draperies, and shades for the same reason.

•Be sure vinyl and bare floors are freshly washed (not waxed—you don't want your prospective buyers slipping).

•Neaten up the basement and attic. Wipe up any water, including water from around the sink or the washing machine.

•Is there a fireplace? If it's winter and the fireplace works well (you know best), light a fire. In summer, buy some plants (Boston ferns can look terrific) and put them in the fireplace.

*A neat well-kept appearance will help to sell your home.*

•Keep noise to a minimum when people are going through your house—that means no TV, radio, or record player. This type of noise is distracting and, to many people, annoying. They may not know exactly what bothered them, but they will remember there was something they didn't like about your house.

## Preliminary Planning

Doing some preliminary planning on your move is one way to make sure it is less difficult than it might be. This takes time, which may be a problem since your other responsibilities continue despite the fact that you are moving, but it will save you a lot of time and trouble later.

Planning starts with asking yourself some questions.

•How far away is your new home? Is it across the country or the world, or just down the street?

The further you are moving the more time you should allow for the actual physical move. If you are using professional movers it is likely that they will show up at your new home later than expected.

•How ready is your new home?

If you're moving into a new house or apartment, it's just as well not to rely too heavily on the builder's or management's dates as to when your home will be ready. Allow extra time—how much is anybody's guess. You can get a rough estimate by talking to people in the area with experience with the builder or management. Obviously, if there's a problem like a construction workers' strike you'll be delayed by the length of the strike, but a great many other problems can arise, from cold weather to a lumber shortage. If you are moving to a new place that is not yet finished, and you can possibly afford it, consider carrying two homes for a while. It's expensive, but it beats having to stay in a motel.

• The question of the readiness of your new home is also important if you are moving into an existing house, apartment, or mobile home. If the house is empty well in advance of your move (say, six weeks before) you may be able to get started early on painting and wallpapering and things like that if you plan to do them or have them done.

• Is your new home clean?

This doesn't mean cleaner than clean, as some people think, just clean by your standards. Even if it is clean by your standards, you may want to give everything a good going over while it's empty just because you may never have as good a chance again. Obviously, if the house is miles away from where you are now, or if someone else is still living in it, this opportunity won't arise, and you may well find yourself doing the cleaning with all the furniture in place.

• How will you move?

This is the time to plan (roughly) how you and everyone else in your family and all the things you all have accumulated over the years will be moved. In the next chapter, we go into actually deciding the method of moving.

• Do you want to move yourself? How? Do you want to move with a mover? Do you want to move fast, with an all-out effort by everyone (many people say it's the best way), or slowly (if you have the option)?

• How carefully do you want to move? Do you have a lot of things that, because of value or sentiment, you want to be sure don't get broken in the move? Or do you feel that you have to expect a few breakages in moving, and refuse to get excited at the thought? Your answers to these questions will play a large role in determining how you pack.

• How much do you want to move?

The easiest way to move, after all, is by picking up a suitcase and walking out the door, leaving the accumulations of the years behind. Some people who move great distances—to other countries, for instance— often throw out everything they can't carry with them and start over. It's a thought. In any case, if you can afford it, now is the time to throw out the sofa with the broken springs. Buy a new one when you're in your new home.

• How much can you spend to move? Whose money will it be?

Moving firms must jump with joy every time organizations that pay for moves transfer people. It's inevitable that people will move more if the company is paying for everything (and that means everything, including packing) than if the individuals are paying for the move themselves.

## Finding a Place to Live

To help narrow down your choice of new homes and, if you are working with a real estate agent, to give the agent a better idea of what you want in a home, indicate on the chart opposite your feelings about the various subjects.

|  | Important | Unimportant |
|---|---|---|
| House |  |  |
| Apartment |  |  |
| Other (mobile home, etc.) |  |  |
| Good schools |  |  |
| Politics of area |  |  |
| Nearness to town |  |  |
| Degree of privacy |  |  |
| Availability of ethnic foods |  |  |
| Mortgage availability |  |  |

## House vs. Apartment

**Apartment**  Size (usually smaller than house)
Lack of yard (and yard work)
Nearness of neighbors
Lack of stairs (usually)
Tenant usually does not do repairs
or maintenance

**House**  Size (usually larger than apartment)
Yard
Privacy
Storage space

## Selling Your Home

**Agent**    Saves your time
             Can arrive at realistic price
             Can advise on making home more salable
             Saves you from emotional problems of selling
             Brings buyer and seller together

**Multiple**  As above, although some feel agents work
**listing**   harder if listing is exclusive; in
             theory, many agents working to sell
             your home

**Yourself**  Save agent's commission
             Can set own appointments with
             prospective buyers rather than
             having home always ready

# 2

# CHOOSING HOW
# TO MOVE

When most of us think of moving, we tend to think of huge moving vans outside a house being loaded up with everything. While this is one of the most common methods of moving, it is certainly not the only one. You may be able to save money by moving another way or by a combination of ways. In any case, you should consider all the possibilities so you'll be sure you're using the best method for you.

If your company is paying for your move, saving money will probably not be as important to you as it would be if you were paying for the move yourself. Before you assume that an organization is paying for everything, find out exactly what is included. Will the organization pay for packing and unpacking as well as for the moving? Will the organization pay for everything—but only up to a certain total dollar limit? While some organizations will pay every penny of a move resulting from a transfer, others will pay as little as $100.

If your company is not paying for your move, there are several ways to move that will save you money. While some of these methods involve trading either your time or your strength for money, most are simply a

matter of knowing about and then choosing the right
method to move certain things.

## Moving Yourself

Moving yourself is, of course, the most economical
method, although it can be somewhat costly in terms of
frayed tempers. It works best for people who are
traveling fairly light—for instance, moving the contents
of a small apartment a relatively short distance. If the
driving time between the two homes is more than, say,
half an hour, it becomes difficult simply because of the
time it will take to make trips back and forth.

Moving yourself starts with packing for yourself,
since if you're doing your own transporting you're
probably not going to be hiring anyone to do the
packing. Small items (dishes, books, records) go into
boxes. Large items (beds, mattresses, sofas, rugs) travel
on their own, perhaps covered with old sheets or large
pieces of brown wrapping paper.

If you have very few belongings you may be able to
move using a station wagon (rented or borrowed), but
you may find a van better.

While you'll probably be able to rent a station wagon
with your regular license, you may need another type of
license to rent a van. This is something that varies from
state to state and from rental agency to rental agency;
it's something to check out well in advance. If you
really have a lot to move, you may want to rent a
truck—if, of course, you have some experience driving
trucks and a license that permits it. One trip is always
better than two or more trips, although you may have to
make more than one in the end.

If you're under 25 you may have difficulty renting any kind of vehicle (perhaps an over-25 friend will rent and drive for you). Many rental agencies require a hefty deposit (around $200 in cash) if you don't have a credit card, and many won't rent to you at all unless you have a credit card.

Moving yourself works best for short moves and on moves where relatively few possessions are involved. In any case, moving yourself is physically tiring and the more help you can get the better. Before you decide to definitely move yourself, consider the fact that it is time consuming. If you feel you would rather not trade your time and muscle for money, choose another moving method.

Load a station wagon placing small items inside the car. Larger items can be tied firmly to the car roof with rope.

## LOADING UP

Load up the inside of a station wagon with the boxes containing the small items. Put a mattress on top of the car with a box spring on top of that, both tied firmly to the roof with rope. Rugs travel the same way unless they are small enough to fit inside.

Bureaus, desks, chairs, and sofas will sometimes fit inside a station wagon—especially if they can be taken apart or, at least, have the legs unscrewed. Sometimes these things will have to ride on the top, too, which means a lot of trips back and forth—which is why a van or truck is better if you have a lot to move.

## WORKING WITH YOUR HELPERS

Try to con your friends and relatives into helping you move if you possibly can. You probably need at least three people to move such things as sofas and bureaus without getting exhausted—and more is better, so people can rest.

Be as ready as possible when your helpers arrive and know exactly how you want things moved. Decide ahead of time, for instance, whether you want the beds to go out first or the living room cleared first.

Don't forget that you'll also have to offer your helpers both food and drink. Beer or soft drinks are traditional for moving; don't give your helpers hard liquor, because it tends to slow people down. Don't try to prepare food yourself. For one thing, you want the pots and pans clean for the move, and for another, you'll be much too busy. Good sandwiches from the best delicatessen in town may be expensive, but they keep your work crew from disappearing to find something to eat. Figure on four sandwiches per person, including yourself and other family members. You can always eat any left-overs in your new home. Use paper plates and paper cups so there won't be any dirty dishes.

Don't pack your ashtrays until everything and everyone is out of your old home. You don't want to move out leaving a lot of cigarette butts behind.

## Using a Local Trucker

If you don't want to do your own moving and are not moving out of your state, you can often save money by using a local trucker. Moving companies going outside of the state are subject to the regulations of the Interstate Commerce Commission; local truckers are not, although some are subject to intrastate regulations. In some states, for instance, while interstate movers who are subject to ICC regulations must charge by weight and distance, truckers who do not go out of state may charge either by weight and distance or by time. In many cases, paying by the hour will prove less expensive than paying by weight, especially if you have things well organized in advance of the move.

In fairly large metropolitan areas you'll probably find two types of local truckers—organized amateurs and professionals.

The amateurs (who usually have other professions that have not yet proved profitable) are not as amateurish as you might expect. In most cases they are very experienced and know how to carry, load, and unload efficiently. Many people who have used these "amateurs" say it's almost like using your friends, only better.

If you work with a professional trucker (not a mover) you will probably pay more for your move than if you use amateurs, but you may very well not get more. Some professional truckers seem to feel that they have seen a lot of different things come and go and there is no reason to take very much care with your things. Others seem to require a great deal of sympathy, telling tales of other people they've worked for who weren't fair, or how often the truck breaks down, before they're prepared to go to work. Talk to as many people as you can for advice on choosing a trucker.

In either case, if you hire a local trucker make sure it's known that you are hiring the truck in order to move. Spell out exactly how far it will be from where the truck will have to park to your new home. Nothing makes people crosser than finding out unexpectedly that they have to carry a breakfront up 28 steps.

## Professional Interstate Movers

Interstate movers come under the jurisdiction of the Interstate Commerce Commission.

*Local truckers are experienced, efficient, and usually less expensive to use than moving companies.*

A great many of the rules regulating the moving industry (tariffs) seem to benefit the mover rather than the consumer. However, spurred by the consumer movement and criticism, the Commission seems to be trying to put its house in order and certain things are now required of movers that benefit consumers.

While enforcement of the regulations isn't yet what it should be, there is no question but that the Commission is trying harder to do its job and is following up on complaints better. That's why it's important for people who have experiences with movers that are less than satisfactory to let the ICC know.

## INTERSTATE COMMERCE COMMISSION RULES

Among the most important of the Interstate Commerce Commission rules for the consumer are the following:

• Your goods must be weighed on scales that have been certified by the municipal or county Bureau of Weights and Measures. You must be allowed to watch the weighing.

• The estimate of the cost of the move must be based on actual inspection of your goods at your home.

• The mover must give you the ICC booklet *Summary of Information for Shippers of Household Goods* before you sign what is called an Order for Service (that is, an agreement to have this particular mover do the move).

• The mover must give you the Order for Service before moving day. It must have on it the estimated price quoted and the dates the moving van will pick up and deliver (the mover may legally make you agree to a span of days—say, June 1 to 5).

• The moving van must come on the day promised, or within the span of days agreed on. If it doesn't, the

moving company can be fined up to $500. This doesn't
help you much because you don't get the money, but it
does tend to discourage movers from taking a cavalier
attitude toward dates.

• The mover must deliver your goods and do anything
else requested (such as putting the furniture where you
want it, putting things back together if they were taken
apart for the move, unpacking) as soon as you pay the
amount estimated, plus no more than an additional 10%
when there's been a gross underestimate.

• The cost of packing and unpacking must be itemized
separately on the bill, and you need not pay for unpacking unless you have ordered it. If you've ordered it and
the mover refuses to do the unpacking (this is quite
common) you get a refund, or will if you fight for it.

*Professional interstate movers are subject to the regulations
of the Interstate Commerce Commission.*

• In addition to spelling out the regulations so that they are more in favor of the customer, the ICC now has a program for judging moving companies.

Companies are required to show figures for the previous year indicating how often they were late with either pickups or deliveries, the percentage of moves in which there was an underestimate of costs of more than 10%, how often claims over $50 were filed against the company, and how long it took the company to settle the claims.

Each moving company must give you its own performance record for the previous year when the estimator arrives to estimate. This is just one of the reasons why you should talk to more than one moving company—so you can compare performance records.

There is a hitch in all this—the companies supply the information on which the performance record is based. The ICC does blow the whistle when it finds companies being a little too kind to themselves, but despite this you can't expect the information to be entirely impartial.

The use of the performance record becomes more complicated when you realize that many major moving companies work through independent agents in various communities. This means that a company's overall record can be terrific but, if the agent where you live is not up to standard, you'd be better off not using that company.

How do you find out about your local agent? Well, in addition to getting estimates from more than one company, you should make a point of talking to as many people as you can about their experiences in moving. If you find people consistently say a certain company is really excellent, that is certainly a company that you should put at the top of your list.

As we said earlier, when most of us think of moving we think of moving with a big moving van. If you're moving quite a distance across the country, you'll probably find that you have to use one of these movers.

While there are truckers who will cross state lines who are not licensed to do so, they are actually breaking the law by defying ICC regulations. If anything happens to your goods while they are being moved by such a trucker, you would find it very difficult and perhaps impossible to collect any money.

How will you be charged? Rather than charging by the hour, as many truckers do, the moving companies' charges are based on the weight of your household goods and the distance traveled. Be prepared to find many additional charges—for instance, 50¢ or more per 100 pounds if an elevator is involved, about 25¢ per 100 pounds for each flight of stairs, and an extra charge around the $25 mark if a piano or organ comes into the picture.

Before the moving company will make an appointment to move you, someone from the company will have to make an estimate. These estimates tend not to be worth much, but if they are just given lightly over the telephone they are worth even less. Although the ICC regulations require the estimator to actually look at your goods, occasionally one will try to skip this step. Don't permit it.

When the estimator comes to your home be sure he or she looks at, around, and under everything. Make clear what you are leaving behind and what you are taking— major appliances, for instance, weigh a great deal and whether or not they are being moved can affect the estimate.

By looking at the household goods you have, the estimator will figure out the approximate cost of the move based on the weight and the distance.

The movers will give you an estimate but it's only that—it's not a bid. If the move costs less than the estimate, because your goods weigh less than figured, you'll pay less. If the move costs more than the estimate, you'll pay more.

Movers are not allowed to unload your household possessions until charges have been paid. They are also not "allowed" to accept personal checks—even though they will, presumably, be able to find you again if the check bounces. Instead, you must pay with cash, a money order, a cashier's check, or traveler's checks.

## PAYING THE MOVERS

The moving company may try to tell you that you must pay the full amount, including any amount above the estimate, before the truck is unloaded. This isn't true.

You do have to pay the full amount eventually, but you only have to pay immediately 10% of the amount over the estimate if the estimate was low. This isn't wonderful, but it's better than having to find the full amount if the estimate was very far off the mark.

How do you prepare to pay what is usually a very large sum of money—$2000 is a good guess for an average household going about a thousand miles—when you can't pay by personal check and don't know the full amount?

One of the most efficient ways is to carry with you and have ready a cashier's check or a certified check for the amount of the estimate. Then, in traveler's checks, have 10% more than the estimate. Be sure to have some relatively small traveler's checks ($10's and $20's) so there won't be a lot of trouble about making change.

Of course, if you want, there's no real reason why you shouldn't pay the full amount of your move (if it's no more than 10% over the estimate) on the day your goods arrive.

You have 15 working days to pay the balance on an underestimate—Saturday, Sunday, and holidays don't count.

To be fair to moving companies, the underestimates of weight don't seem to be deliberate. Moving companies are about equally likely to overestimate the cost of a move as to underestimate it.

## Moving by Air

Have you ever thought about moving by air? It won't really work for your whole move unless you have a minimum of items, but you'll probably be surprised at how much you can take with you on a plane.

Rules and regulations about luggage keep changing in the airline industry, so your first step will be to find out exactly what the permitted sizes are and how much you're allowed to take with you. You'll probably find there's no limit to what you can take if you're willing to pay, and that the cost will be quite reasonable.

Let's say you're moving from Los Angeles to New York. The figures that follow were correct at the time this book was written, but think of them as round figures rather than definite regulations and check before you pack.

On domestic flights you're allowed to have with you one piece of carry-on luggage (45 inches overall, which means height plus width plus depth) weighing not more than 70 pounds.

In addition, you can check through, free, two other pieces of luggage—one 62 inches (measured the same as above) and the other 55 inches (again measured the same way). Neither of these can weigh more than 70 pounds.

In addition to the free things you can take with you, a package measuring no more than 80 inches (measured the same way) and not weighing more than 70 pounds can make the trip with you for only $5. A larger, heavier package will cost you $10. This can weigh up to 150 pounds, must not measure more than 72 inches in any single direction and no more than a total of 160 inches nor less than a total of 81 inches.

Use large sturdy cartons for packing (appliance stores often have just what you need) and cut them to

*Moving long distances by air might be the most economical.*

size if necessary. Things such as chairs, tables, and desks should be taken apart as much as possible so they'll fit the airline size regulations.

Don't try to take all your household goods to the airport in a taxi—find a friend with a van and a willing spirit to help you, at both ends of the trip if possible. Use porters, if any, and tip lavishly to ease your conscience about the bulk of your luggage.

Check in for your flight well in advance (you might tell the airline how much luggage you'll have, and ask them what the best time for check-in is).

Keep in mind those pictures you've seen of movie stars arriving with heaven only knows how many suitcases and trunks. The more people who are moving with you, of course, the better, as each one can take this much "luggage;" but no matter what, your expenses will be surprisingly modest.

## MIXING METHODS

This brings us to one of the main points we want to make about moving. The best way to move may not actually be any single way, but rather several ways.

For instance, you probably won't be able to take most of your appliances by air—they'll be both too large and too heavy. If you feel you want to move them they should probably go by moving van.

And there's an alternative to both those methods, too. You can move things by bus, although not very much. You probably don't have to go along, although it's cheaper in many cases if you do. Different bus companies have different charges and customs and size regulations. These rules, like those of the airlines, are very much subject to change. One bus company, for instance, will accept packages up to 150 pounds in weight, measuring 141 inches overall (you know, that height, weight, and depth measurement) with no single measurement more than 72 inches. Charges are determined by distance your packages are going and the size; if you're going to send them about 200 miles figure each package will cost you under $10. This, of course, can change.

The biggest saving in using an alternate means of sending some of your household goods—and the further you go the more you will save—is on books, records, and tapes. These can all be mailed and you can save a bundle doing so. These items are classified now by the post office as being in the Special 4th Class Rate group (formerly called the Educational Materials group). This is a parcel post class but, unlike other parcel post classes, with the Special 4th Class Rate there is no zoning—the postage is the same no matter how far you are sending the things. Again, postage rates change so much that it would be misleading to give you rates for mailing by Special 4th Class Rate, but you'll be safe to figure between 10¢ and 20¢ the pound (not ounce like 1st Class Mail). Check the maximum weight, too, before packing your books and records and so forth. It may be as much as 70 pounds but, since you'll have to get the boxes to the post office, you may want to limit the weight to 50 pounds, about as much as the average nonprofessional can be expected to lift without trouble.

While the Special 4th Class Rate is one of the all-time bargains for people on the move, you don't have to limit your mailing of things to your new address to that category. Using regular parcel post you can mail things that are bulky but light in weight, such as curtains and out-of-season clothes. Again, check the post office for the latest regulations and then weigh your package at home to be sure it meets the requirements.

## Possible Moving Methods

**Yourself** Economical; time consuming; physically tiring (get help); best if move is local

**Local trucker** Economical (as compared to professional movers); most local truckers are experienced in household moving; usually takes less time than moving yourself would

**Moving van** Fairly expensive; movers are extremely experienced in moving household goods; usually takes less time than moving yourself would

**Airplane** Fairly economical for distance traveled, speed of trip, fact that goods arrive with you; limited number of items fit into height and weight specifications

**Bus** As for airplane, above

**Mail** Most economical method of all for anything (books, records, tapes) qualifying for Special 4th Class Rate

# 3

# STARTING TO PACK

Once you've worked out how you are going to move the actual work will take relatively little time.

Packing, however, can be—or seem—almost endless.

You can arrange to have the movers do all the packing for you, but this is quite expensive. The charge is figured on the basis of the box or other container plus the labor. The box can easily cost you about $3 while the labor can be as much as $10 per container. If you do decide to have the movers pack for you, figure that it will cost you about $500—you may be pleasantly surprised and discover it is less.

You can keep that price lower by not having the movers do all the packing. You may want to pack your more fragile possessions yourself, or rely on the movers to pack them, or simply divide things by room with the movers packing some and you packing others. Get a price for this in advance, when the estimator comes.

The least expensive way of all, of course, is to make it an entirely do-it-yourself job. While this does take time, many people prefer it on the grounds that they then know their things are packed the way they want.

## Weeding Out

Before you start, work on the question of what can be eliminated. Don't get carried away and throw out the relics of a lifetime, but do take stock of things that can and probably should be tossed out. Think about having a garage sale—there may be someone in your community who sets up, publicizes, and sells at garage sales for a fee; check into this. You can also give things to charity or to friends.

Establish some ground rules about the throwing out and packing in general at a family meeting, or at dinner, or just by shouting back and forth on a Saturday morning. If possible, try to work things out so that everyone is responsible for weeding out his or her own possessions.

*Make your move easier by eliminating what you no longer want or need before you pack.*

There has to be a certain degree of unanimity about "family" possessions. To keep peace, it's not a bad idea to have a pile of things to be thrown out somewhere in the house so that people can rush in and rescue things that other people felt were no longer needed.

This weeding may not be a problem for you. Some people keep a great deal more than other people simply from a sort of inertia, while others who live a very stripped-down kind of life won't have much—if anything—to clean out.

Here are some points to keep in mind.

● Don't pack things you've been meaning to get rid of for years just because you're so used to seeing them. Enough of these and you've added a substantial amount of weight and probably expense to your move.

● Don't throw out any child's toy—however dirty and unappealing it may be.

● Don't decide that someone else doesn't need, doesn't use, or doesn't want something else. Just knowing something is there gives lots of people a warm feeling.

● Everyone should agree on how much is to be thrown out. It's not fair to have one person weeding out his or her property while everyone else moves everything.

## THE THINGS YOU DON'T WANT

Work out how you are going to get rid of things that the family no longer wants.

Are you going to have a garage sale? If so, you might get some idea of what the price for various things in your area is by going to other people's garage sales so you won't price yourself too low or too high.

At the same time, keep in mind that the purpose of your particular garage sale is to clear out the things you won't be moving. There's no point in keeping the price up to a certain standard you've set for yourself if you are just going to have to put the things in the garbage.

Give your friends a chance to look over the leftovers from your garage sale. You may find they've always admired something you've hated for years.

Garage sales can be nice and bring you in a bit of change (although probably not as much as you would hope for), but they do take time away from other things you might want to do, such as pack or go through other things. At least one family member or friend has to watch the garage sale to be sure no one walks off with anything and to take the money of those who want to pay. In some areas there are people who have made a profession of running garage sales and this, as we said earlier, is certainly worth looking into.

*A garage sale is a good way to eliminate the things you no longer want and at the same time earn money.*

You may not want to have a garage sale but instead decide to give your discards to charity. While the tendency is to think that a charity will come and pick up what you want to give it, you may find that this is not always the case. In fact, although most charities advertise that they will pick up from you, when you ask for a pickup you may be told it can't be made for six weeks and then only if the things you're giving are of fairly high quality. The easiest solution would be to just put the things in your car and drive them to the charity, but sometimes there is just too much, sometimes you have no car, and sometimes (especially when you are moving) you have no time. A less-than-charitable treatment of the charity by you can, on occasion, have a good effect. A simple "Oh, well, in that case I'll put it all in the garbage" is good but we've found a suggestion that it will be given to another charity works even better.

This is certainly not the attitude of all charities that are willing to take things, but it is something you should be prepared to handle if the situation arises. Be sure to label everything with your name and new address so the charity can send you a credit for use with your income tax if you don't take the standard deduction.

## Starting to Pack

If you have a great many things (hundreds of records, thousands of books, small figurines, and so forth) you should start packing as soon as possible. Four to six weeks before the move is not too early if you have somewhere to put the packed boxes that won't be too much in your way.

If you are using a moving company, don't buy the packing materials from the agent and don't rent containers from the agent. Charges are high for these things compared to other sources (especially compared to getting them for nothing), and they are no better. Liquor store and furniture store cartons are highly recommended for moving by many people, as are the cartons that large amounts of photocopier paper come in. For records, get cartons from your record dealer.

Most cartons are labeled to show how strong they are according to "burst strength." Look for at least 200 lbs. burst strength for small cartons and 275 lbs. burst strength for larger ones. Burst strength is a term that indicates the weight a carton can bear.

You'll save money if you mail your books and records at the Special 4th Class Rate as we said in the last chapter. If you are moving far, mail books and records about two weeks before you move; if you're going to somewhere fairly close, wait to mail them until a day or two before the actual move.

## The Packing

Here is how to pack various specific items.

*Books*—Pack books with the spines (the part that gives the title and author) going in alternate directions. Stuff newspaper into every place you can before sealing the box.

Avoid cramming the books together as this puts a strain on the spine. The newspaper is needed because even the best-bound book is likely to show signs of strain if it is tumbled around inside a carton.

*Records*—Using record cartons from your record store, pack your records. Try also to get from the record store corrugated cardboard (it comes with the record boxes) that fits the boxes. You should use two pieces of this cardboard for each record box. Put one piece of the corrugated cardboard on the bottom of the box, pack the records (you don't need cardboard between the records), and put the last piece of cardboard on top of the records. Tape the box closed.

If you have no record store near you, you can use the other cartons you've managed to acquire, such as ones from the liquor store, but you'll have to cut them down so they are no more than six inches high or they will be too heavy to lift when packed and probably too heavy for the post office to accept. Again, use corrugated cardboard on top and bottom or, if necessary, newspaper.

*Pack books with spines in alternate directions.*

*China and Glass*—It will go on the moving van or by whatever other means you're using to move your household goods. You might, however, want to take it along in the car if it is very valuable for reasons of age or sentiment.

Moving companies will tell you they aren't responsible for your china and glass if they don't do the packing, but many people who have moved several times have found they had much less breakage when they did the packing themselves than when they let the movers do it for them.

Wrap china and glass carefully in newspaper. Put an inch or two of newspaper at the bottom of each box as a cushion, then pack it in boxes with plenty of other newspaper around it for protection. Pack the heaviest pieces at the bottom of the box, the medium weight in the middle, and the lightest on top. Mark the box to show which end is up.

It's not worthwhile washing dusty china and glass before you pack it unless you have lots of time and won't have any later. Instead, plan to wash such rarely used pieces in your new home after the newspaper wrapping and the effects of the move.

As an extra protection for glasses, stuff paper into them (not too tightly or they'll break) to support them and keep them from being crushed.

Label the box and mark it "Fragile."

*Rugs and Carpets*—If you live near enough to your new home, have the rugs and carpets cleaned before you move and have them delivered to your new home when you're ready. If you're moving too far to do this, roll up the rugs and carpets a day or two before the move to get them out of the way and keep them as clean as possible.

Movers seem to have dirtier feet than you might expect and there's no point getting your rugs dirtied. For the same reason, if you have rugs cleaned and delivered to your new home don't put them down until the movers leave.

*Curtains, Draperies, Shades, Blinds*—Most people leave their shades and blinds in the old home (it's almost impossible to adjust these so they'll fit new windows), but take their curtains and draperies with them in the hope that they can use them in the new location. Don't, however, assume that the person moving out of the place you're moving into will leave the shades and blinds behind. Ask.

*Wrap china and glass carefully in newspaper. Place the heaviest items at the bottom of the carton, the lightest on top.*

If you are sending your curtains or draperies out to be cleaned, arrange to have them delivered to your new home if possible. In your new home is too far away, wrap them in brown paper (newspaper might dirty them) and then put them in one of your boxes.

If you know your old curtains and draperies won't fit your new windows or if you want a change, try to get the measurements of your new windows before you move so the new draperies and curtains can be in the works early. Make sure the measuring is done accurately (this means carefully) and that every window is

*Most people leave window shades, but take their curtains and draperies with them.*

measured individually. Don't make the mistake of as-
suming that all windows in a room or home are the
same size just because they look the same.

*Fragile Lamps, Vases, China Accessories*—Wrap in
newspaper. Put a layer of newspaper on the bottom of
a box, pack the items, then add another layer of
newspaper. Large floor lamps will fit in refrigerator
cartons. Whether or not you take the bulbs out of the
lamps is up to you. Some people do, others don't. The
ones who don't feel that transporting individual bulbs
is as awkward as transporting bulbs in lamps.

*Lampshades*—Lampshades should be wrapped in tissue
paper or brown wrapping paper rather than newspaper
to avoid getting them marked. Try to find boxes that fit
each lampshade with a little extra room on the sides.
You may find your lampshades nest together; in that
case, wrap and pack two as one.

*Silverware*—You should probably take sterling silver
with you as part of your luggage. Put sterling silver in
silvercloth bags if you have them, or wrap it, a few
pieces at a time, in tissue paper or clean fabric, and then
put it in a box. If you have a silver chest, of course, you
can put that in your luggage with your silver in it.

*Pictures and Mirrors*—Pictures and mirrors can be
moved either individually or in boxes, depending on
size. Smaller ones can be wrapped in lots of newspaper
and put into boxes, while very large mirrors should be
wrapped in paper, tied with strong twine, and labeled
"Fragile."

   If you own any valuable paintings these should not
be left to regular movers. Either carry a valuable

painting with you or arrange for it to be crated and shipped by one of the companies that specialize in moving art objects for museums and collectors. The same thing goes for any other valuable work of art you may have, such as a piece of sculpture.

*Kitchen Pots and Pans*—Kitchen pots and pans don't cook well if they get banged around too much, so treat them the way you treat the more obviously fragile things you own. Wrap them in newspaper, then pack them in cartons with a layer of newspaper on the bottom and additional layers between each kitchen item.

*Mattresses and Box Springs*—Mattresses and box springs should be protected in a move from getting dirty and torn. If you have wrapping paper (not newspaper as it would do its own share of dirtying) large enough, you can wrap the mattresses and box springs in that. If not, large sheets that you aren't using anymore are fine.

*Food*—Whether or not it's worth moving food depends on the distance you are traveling and what the food is. In any case, it's a good idea to have a cutoff date on food purchasing well in advance of the move.

If you're only moving a short distance it's probably worthwhile moving canned foods (not something you bought four years ago and have yet to eat, though) if they're unopened.

Throw out any opened cans or jars of food, any fresh food, and any odds and ends such as a bit of ham or the leftover roast. It's too difficult to keep these foods so they won't mold, spoil, or whatever and poison you.

*Non-upholstered Furniture*—While the packing of those items that go in boxes is time consuming because of the need to wrap almost everything before packing, preparing furniture is much simpler.

On wood furniture, a light coating of paste wax may give more protection than just the furniture pads the movers will use. Don't use furniture polish (it's too oily and won't protect sufficiently) and don't wax heavily (the wax will come off on the movers' furniture pads and make the movers cross).

Whether or not the waxing is worth doing depends on the type of wood furniture you have. You probably would not want to wax Early American furniture, for instance, as the scratches and dents of time are considered part of the beauty of this furniture. Very glossy mahogany furniture, on the other hand, should certainly be protected with such a wax coating.

More and more wood, plastic, and metal furniture these days is being made so that it can fold flat for moving. If you have any of this type of furniture you'll naturally take it apart into its pieces for the move.

*Upholstered Furniture*—Upholstered furniture needs very little preparation for moving. If you're moving yourself, unscrew the legs if they come off and remove the cushions, if any, to pack separately.

*Plants*—Unless you're moving within the same state, and moving only a short distance, plants will prove to be among the most complicated things you will move, not only because they are awkward in shape but because of regulations governing their admission by various states. See Chapter 9, "Moving Plants and Pets," for details.

*Pets*—Pets are usually not much of a problem to move within the United States, but be sure your pet has a health certificate and rabies inoculations from your veterinarian. When you take your pet to the vet, check about the regulations governing your particular pet in the place to which you are moving. In most cases there will be no problem, but some states (Hawaii is one) have strict regulations. See Chapter 9, "Moving Plants and Pets," for more information.

## STORAGE

What about storage? Should you plan to store some of your things in the course of the move?

Storage sometimes seems like a tempting answer to problems ranging from a house that's not ready to a family that isn't able to reach the new home in time to supervise the unloading of a furniture van. If you can avoid storage at all, however, avoid it—even if it means one member of the family has to fly to the new home while the others arrive later.

Why? Storage not only costs money but people who have moved often report they have the greatest loss and damage to their household goods when they are in storage. Yes, of course you can get insurance, but what good is insurance if Great Uncle Will's sideboard is damaged beyond repair?

## LETTING THE MOVERS PACK

This chapter has concerned itself with the way in which you yourself should pack your household goods for a move. If you are using movers, why not let them do the packing for you?

The main reason is expense. Professional movers will charge you for packing, as we mentioned earlier, both by the box or other container and by time. One estimate is that it will cost about $500 to pack the "average sized household," but very few households are really average.

The second reason for doing your own packing is that many people have found that not all professional movers do a good packing job. It's frustrating to watch someone you are paying pack badly when you know that you yourself could do a better job.

It probably does make sense to have the movers pack if your organization is paying for your entire move (including packing) and if you or some other conscientious person can spare the time to watch the packing in operation. Otherwise, you'd be wise to ensure the quality of the packing by doing it yourself.

## Special Preparations

If you can, check out the major-appliance situation— refrigerator, stove, dishwasher, washing machine, dryer. Take a metal tape measure or a metal ruler with you so you can measure spaces and compare the space available with the size of the appliances.

This is important (and tricky) in the case of a kitchen for which you have to supply the appliances if the kitchen was designed around the space required by the previous occupant's appliances.

When do appliances go and when do they stay?

In most cases the basic appliances are supplied with a rented house or apartment, but are not supplied with a purchased house or apartment. If you are buying a house or apartment and don't own appliances already, you might want to ask the present owners if they want to throw their old ones in with the purchase—that is, if they fit a special place, are not very old, seem to work well, and you like their looks.

Wall-to-wall carpeting usually stays, whether the house or apartment is rented or owned. Don't assume that it will be staying, however, and don't pay for it unless you have really looked at it and know it's in good condition. Don't buy it either if you hate the color or texture—but that should go without saying.

In any case, whether you're talking about carpeting or appliances, be sure you're in command of the situation when someone else is trying to sell them to you. These things depreciate fast. Don't make more than a token payment for them. Check the secondhand ads in a newspaper to get some idea of how much would be fair.

## PREPARING APPLIANCES

If you are not leaving your appliances behind and they are moving any distance, they will be your first headache when it comes to packing.

This is because certain appliances may need to be bolted, tied, wedged, and so forth before being moved so they won't shake apart (or at least shake enough so they won't work after the move). The term usually used to describe getting these appliances ready for their move is "servicing"—not to be confused with servicing an appliance that breaks down.

Some appliances, such as small appliances, don't need any servicing for moving. Tape down or remove any knobs on these, however. See the chart on preparing appliances to move.

Moving companies and appliance manufacturers don't agree entirely about how appliances should be prepared for moving. The moving companies have quite elaborate ideas of what you should do or have done (and they'll get someone to do it for you or do it themselves) while most appliance handbooks barely mention the subject. This is really a case where you will have to decide for yourself. If you do decide to have certain appliances serviced, have it done by the representative from the manufacturer rather than by the movers.

Start your moving of appliances by making sure they are clean and dry. The cleanliness is so that, in the case of a refrigerator for example, there won't be a smell from decayed bits of food if the movers deliver your things late.

The dryness is essential because otherwise you may well have a nice little growth of mold and mildew—and pretty revolting that is, too, as well as being almost impossible to get rid of in terms of stain and smell.

There's another important reason for trying to be sure that your appliances are dry, and that is that in cold weather there's a good chance that any water might freeze, expand, and damage the appliance.

If your stove is very greasy it should be cleaned thoroughly, as grease can turn rancid and gum up or dirty anything it touches.

Here are specific steps for cleaning various items in preparation for a move.

*Refrigerator and/or Freezer*—Start by planning your life so that you will have used up everything in the refrigerator about two days before the move. If you don't manage, you can give a lot to your neighbors and friends or have a non-stop eat-everything-in-the-refrigerator meal.

Unplug the refrigerator or freezer and defrost it. If your refrigerator has either an automatic ice maker or a cold water dispenser (or both), be sure these are empty of water before you try to move the appliance.

To be extra sure that nothing gets banged around in the move you can take out things like shelves, meat trays, ice cube trays, and so forth and pack them separately, but it probably isn't really necessary.

Wash the refrigerator or freezer with detergent solution or baking soda and dry it thoroughly. Paper towels or dish towels work fine. Leave the door open so the refrigerator or freezer will have a chance to dry out further.

Pull it away from the wall and vacuum all those places that are dusty because you've never had a chance to vacuum them before. This is so the dust from these appliances won't be taken out of your present home, carried miles, and delivered to your new home.

When you're ready to move your refrigerator or freezer, tape the door closed so it won't fly open accidentally. Wind the cord on itself and tape it to the back of the refrigerator or freezer.

*Iron*—There is no difficulty with an ordinary iron—just make sure it is cool enough to pack, wind the cord around it, and pack it in a box with a lot of newspaper surrounding it.

If your iron is a steam iron, it's a little more complicated but not terribly difficult. Your main concern in moving it will be to move it dry—partly so no water will spill out by accident, and partly to avoid having it get filled with mildew in case your shipment gets stuck somewhere. Check your instruction book for how to do this properly. If your instruction book has disappeared, here are two methods to use to dry out your steam iron.

You can either pour out the water that is in it and then, changing the setting to "dry," iron for an hour or two; or you can put the iron on some kind of surface

with holes (a cake rack is ideal) over another surface
that heat (the iron will be hot) and dampness (the steam
coming out) won't harm. Set the iron to steam and to the
highest setting and let it run for about 45 minutes or so.

After using either of these methods, let the iron cool
down before packing it. Leave plenty of time for that
particular step—it's amazing how long it takes an iron
to cool when you're in a hurry. Lastly, pack the iron in a
box with or without other items with plenty of newspaper surrounding it.

*Turntable*—Among the most fragile items in your home
is the turntable to your stereo or record player. The
better the turntable, the more delicate it is—the delicate
balance of the turntable is what produces the
distortion-free sound you want.

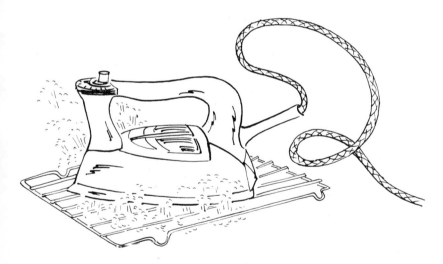

*To get a steam iron dry enough for packing, place it on a
surface with holes such as a cake rack, set it to steam and the
highest setting, and leave it on for 45 minutes. Pack the iron
after it cools.*

This will be easiest to pack if you kept the screws and packing material that came with the turntable and, of course, the instructions for putting it all together. If you did keep these things, you're in luck. Reverse the instructions and you're set to move.

If you didn't keep these things—and lots of people don't, for one reason or another—you'll have to improvise unless you remember pretty well how your turntable was prepared for shipping to you.

Check to see if there are holes for screws that once secured the chassis to the base plate. To find out, lift off the turntable platter (the part you put the records on) and pack that separately. If you don't want to detach the turntable platter for some reason, tape it—the important thing is to keep it from moving during the move.

Do you see any screw holes in the base? (You'll probably see four or five such holes.) The next step— and it may be a real problem, because these screw holes are sometimes very strange sizes—is to find screws. Measure the hole and see what your hardware store can do. If your hardware store can't help, you'll have to try the manufacturer of your turntable to find the screws you need. If you're very lucky, you'll have a compassionate hi-fi shop near you that will help you out. Insert the screws and tighten.

Put the dustcover on the base of your turntable and fasten it firmly all around with tape. Pack this carefully but firmly, using lots of newspaper or clothing or quilts or blankets so that it won't jiggle around.

*Hi-Fi Components*—The rest of your high fidelity components are a good deal less difficult than the turntable to protect from harm.

Speakers, for instance, should be boxed and surrounded by protective material, unless you want to try wrapping them in blankets or rags and treating them as a piece of furniture.

The tuner should be packed carefully. Either remove or tape all the knobs and buttons so they won't be knocked off or broken off. The tuner would probably be securest in a box with a lot of packing material so that it won't shift and risk damage.

The pickup arm (the part that plays the records) should also be fastened down so that it won't swing and move. Again, if you don't have the original packing material, do this with tape.

*Range*—What should you do to the range? We mentioned cleaning it earlier, but this doesn't mean you have to clean the oven or anything like that unless it's really disgusting.

Check the grates and so forth and if they are pretty bad, soak them in detergent solution in the sink, go over them with steel wool, and then either dry them by hand or set them on the stove and light the burners to provide heat for drying them.

You may want to tape certain parts of the range, including the grates and the oven and broiler doors. If you don't plan to move the range with the grates in place, take them off and pack them separately. Also take off the burner knobs so they won't get broken or knocked off, or tape them down, too.

By the way, if you are using a moving company you may find that the movers don't want such things as the grates taken off your stove. Find this out in advance.

*Clothes Washer and Dishwasher*—Clothes washers and dishwashers are treated in very much the same way. Start by disconnecting both from the faucet. Wipe out the inside with a sponge, then dry with paper towels or dish towels. Dry all the various edges and crevices where water can hide, then leave the washer open so that any moisture can evaporate.

The hoses must be drained, of course. Sometimes this is difficult to do—the water won't drain out completely if the hose empties into the sink—and in such a case you should try putting a bucket or pan on the floor and letting the hose drain into that rather than trying to get it to empty out into a sink. It may not be possible to get all the water out even then, but at least you've tried. Again, do this a day or two ahead of your move so it will have a little additional time to dry.

Both clothes washers and dishwashers should be cleaned thoroughly once you're in your new house in case something awful got inside while they were on the road.

To wash, hook them up, then run them through their cycles (but with neither clothes nor dishes in them) in a solution of chlorine bleach (1 teaspoon for the dishwasher, whatever you use for clothes for the clothes washer) or ¼ cup of citric acid crystals (try the drugstore) for the dishwasher. For the clothes washer you can also use baking soda.

The clothes washer will probably need to be serviced for the move, which will mean in most cases some kind of bracing or support to keep the tub from moving around during the move.

Dishwashers, on the other hand, usually don't require servicing before moving.

Once you've moved, if it's winter, don't use any appliance that uses hot water until it has warmed up to room temperature. Very hot water can damage a very cold appliance. You'll probably be safe after waiting 24 hours to use your appliance, but to be sure make it 48 hours.

*Air Conditioners*—Many people move room air conditioners. Check the book that came with the appliance (if you've lost the book, check with the manufacturer) to see if there are special instructions about fastening down the compressor for moving. These instructions are usually quite easy to follow and you can probably do this yourself.

*Radio and Television*—Your television set and your radio will probably pose no problems in moving. If you have an antenna that you want to take with you, take it down fairly early in the move so you can do it carefully rather than in a big rush. Take it down yourself if you put it up yourself; if not, have the people who put it up take it down.

Like everything else, your radio and your television should be packed so they will be as protected as possible. Use strong cartons (you may even be able to get cartons from a hi-fi store that are designed for radios and television sets) and plenty of newspaper.

*Small Appliances*—Small appliances (toasters, electric frying pans, mixers, blenders, and so forth) can be moved as is. You may want to clean them if they're terribly greasy but most people find they have enough to do in the course of a move without cleaning everything in sight. Pack these things in boxes using plenty of newspaper.

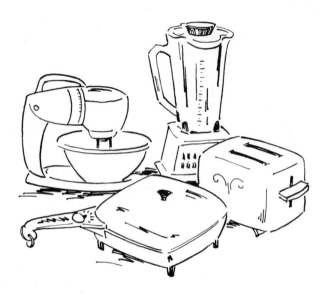

*Small appliances require no special preparation before packing. Simply wrap them in newspaper and pack in boxes.*

Freezer—Unless you are moving a very short distance, forget about taking frozen foods with you. In any case, don't leave them in the freezer to move, not because they'll thaw (although they might) but because the weight of the frozen food itself may break the freezer when it is lifted.

If you do plan to move your frozen foods, you'll be faced with a couple of problems. One of the biggest is the amount of time the foods will have to be out of the freezer while it is being defrosted for the move. Keep the foods wrapped in newspaper until they go back into the freezer and check before putting them back once you are moved to be sure they still have ice crystals and therefore are safe to eat.

If there is a frozen food processing plant near your

old and new homes and you have a great deal of food that is, for one reason or another, valuable to you, find out if you can arrange for it to be stored at the plant until your move is completed and your freezer is once again in action.

Even though freezers aren't really made to move frozen foods, there are 'circumstances under which movers will load a freezer containing frozen foods. If you desperately want to have a full freezer moved by movers, check out these regulations.

These rules have to do with the distance the freezer will travel, the interior temperature of the freezer when it is loaded onto the van, and so on. Of course, one of the most important points of these regulations is that the movers are not responsible for what happens to the food.

*Clocks*—Clocks, and especially grandfather and grandmother clocks, can be a real problem. If you own one, you'll certainly want to move it, but many people tell stories of clocks that ran beautifully until they were moved.

We know of a ship's captain who bought a lovely grandfather clock in England, had it packed very carefully, and then actually had the ship's engines slowed on the Atlantic crossing to try to protect the clock. It didn't work.

In any case, either tape down the pendulum so it won't swing or (if you can) remove it from the clock. And to keep from worrying remember that unless you are living in the first house the clock ever came into, it's probably been moved many times before now—and certainly was moved at least once, when it was brought to your home from the clockmaker or shop.

*Cars, Boats, and Trailers*—Many people who move long distances prefer to fly to their destination but don't want to sell their cars, boats, or trailers before moving. Professional movers will move these things for you, or, in the case of your car, consider using a company that makes a business of driving cars from one end of the country to another. These companies provide what is about the least expensive means of moving your car aside, of course, from driving it yourself.

You will have to prepare your car, boat, or trailer if they are to be moved by a professional mover. This involves the following:

• Be sure the gasoline tank has no more than ¼ of a tankful of gas.

• Be sure there is the right amount of oil in the crankcase so there will be no damage when things are started up at your destination.

• In cold weather or if your vehicle will meet cold weather during its journey, be sure the cooling system has enough antifreeze to protect it.

## Packing Pointers

This chart gives brief pointers for packing various items. For greater detail, and best packing results, see the text.

| | |
|---|---|
| **Books** | Alternate spines, do not cram |
| **Records** | Use record cartons, cardboard top and bottom |
| **China, Glass** | Wrap in newspaper, pack in boxes with newspaper at bottom |

| | |
|---|---|
| **Rugs, Carpets** | Have cleaned, delivered to new home, or roll up for moving |
| **Curtains, Draperies** | Wrap in brown paper, pack in box |
| **Lamps, Vases, etc.** | Wrap in newspaper, pack in box with newspaper layer on bottom |
| **Lampshades** | Wrap in tissue paper or brown wrapping paper |
| **Silver** | Pack in silvercloth or tissue paper or clean fabric, put in box, take with you |
| **Pictures, Mirrors** | Small: wrap in newspaper, pack in boxes; large: wrap in paper, tie with strong twine; valuable paintings: use art specialists |
| **Pots and Pans** | As for china and glass |
| **Mattress, Box Springs** | Cover in wrapping paper or large bed sheets |
| **Wood Furniture** | Give light coating of paste wax if desired— see text |

# Preparing Appliances to Move

| | |
|---|---|
| **Refrigerator and/or Freezer** | Empty, clean, tape door closed, wind cord on itself |
| **Iron** | Empty steam iron, heat until dry |
| **Turntable** | Fasten down—see text |
| **Tuner** | Remove or cover knobs and buttons |
| **Pickup Arm** | Fasten down |
| **Range** | Clean, remove grates or tape down, remove burner knobs or tape down |
| **Clothes Washer** | Drain hose, let dry |
| **Dishwasher** | Drain hose, let dry |
| **Air Conditioner** | Move as is or fasten down compressor; see instruction book or consult manufacturer |
| **Radio, Television** | No special preparations needed |
| **Small Appliances** | No special preparations needed |
| **Clocks** | Tape or remove pendulum |
| **Cars, Boats, Trailers** | Drain all but ¼ tankful of gasoline; be sure crankcase has suffcient oil; be sure cooling system has antifreeze if cold weather |

# Getting Rid of Things You Don't Want

**Garage sale**   Convenient location, possibility of raising money; needs
someone to stay with
merchandise throughout sale;
consider using professional
organizer

**Giving to charity**   Money raised in selling items
will go to a "good cause,"
possibility of credit toward
taxable income deduction;
charity will often request
that you deliver donations

**Throwing out**   Quick, if somewhat extrava-
gant; definitely worth doing
if pressed for time.

# 4

# ORGANIZING A MOVE

Organizing a move so it will go as smoothly as possible takes time and thought, but it is definitely worthwhile. With organization, you are less likely to find that some important step has been overlooked. Without organization, everyone involved is likely to feel overwhelmed by the size of the move.

Organization means setting priorities and doing things in the most efficient way. The following is a suggested timetable for organizing your move.

●If you have children, tell them—even the toddler—about the move as soon as possible. Keep them informed so they'll feel part of what's going on. (See Chapter 5, "Helping the Kids Make the Move.")

●If an organizational transfer is causing your move find out how much, if anything, the organization is prepared to pay toward the move.

In any case, keep a record of every penny you or anyone else in the family spend that is move connected. If your organization isn't paying anything, there's a good chance you can deduct some of your expenses from your income tax. (See Chapter 13, "The Financial Side.")

●Look for your new home. If possible, have at least one member of the family go to the city to which you will be moving for this search. Of course, if the whole family can go it's much better.

If only two people can go, keep in mind that some people have had good luck sending one adult and one child—the child was able to persuade other children in the family that the new place was great.

If it's impossible for anyone in the family to hunt for your new home, find out if the organization you'll be working for can help, check with real estate agents in the city, and use any friends you have there. The advantage of having friends help is that a friend is more likely to tell you the disadvantages of a house or apartment than the real estate agent.

Be sure you are given exact measurements of all the rooms and a drawn layout before you settle on a home.

●If you go house or apartment hunting yourself be sure to have a metal ruler with you to measure rooms if the measurements are not available. It doesn't hurt to spot check any measurements you are given, too. People are sometimes a little optimistic on sizes.

If you're moving your major appliances and desperately want them to look right in your new kitchen and laundry, you should measure to be sure they will fit. It is, however, probably a mistake to turn down a place you really like just because your refrigerator is too tall for the space left under the cabinets. The cabinets can always be moved or changed, or the refrigerator can be put in another spot or replaced.

●If you're buying your new home, arrange financing. If you're selling your old home, make sure all the details of this are worked out correctly. (See Chapter 13, "The Financial Side.")

• If possible, try to allow yourself a full four weeks
between the time you find your new home and the time
you actually move.

## The Next Steps

• Decide how you are going to move. It's likely, if your
organization is paying for everything, that you'll choose
to have a moving company move you and pack, too. If
not, decide how you'll move your various possessions.

• Most people who are moving a distance use professional movers.

Arrange to have two or three agents come to look at
your household goods to give you an estimate on the
move. The estimator will give you an estimate of the
cost of the move which is not binding on you or the
moving company.

• Decide what you want to do about packing. You
may, for instance, want to pack books and records
yourself and let the mover pack everything else, or you
may want the mover to do the whole job, or none of it.

Don't let yourself be frightened into agreeing to
mover packing by hints that the movers aren't liable
unless they do all the packing. They aren't unless you
value your household goods at the highest valuation—
but you should do that in any case.

• Once you have chosen a mover and decided what to
do about packing, arrange to sign an Order for Service.
Don't, of course, sign it until you have read it all. See
also Chapter 8, "Working with the Movers."

• Send change of address cards for magazines as soon
as possible. Magazines usually ask for six weeks notice
but seem to manage with only four. Use cellophane tape
to attach the label from an old copy of each magazine (if

you can find one) for the old address part of the change of address notice. This speeds things up.

Use your Christmas card list and address books to remind you of friends you will want to notify of your move.

• If you're moving quite far away, you probably won't be using your present charge accounts—or not as much. Don't close them, however, unless you're sure you won't want to use them again. You may want to order things by mail. Do notify stores of your new address.

• Start using up all the food that's in the house—the things in the freezer, in the refrigerator, in the storage closet—everything. If you use it up too soon you can always go to the store and buy more.

*Send change of address cards to all magazines that you subscribe to. Attach the mailing label with your old address and mail them at least six weeks before moving.*

• Decide how much of an inventory of your household goods you are going to make. An inventory is a good idea for a move in case things vanish and generally is a good idea for insurance purposes. See Chapter 6, "Taking and Making an Inventory," for the various ways to make one.

• It's a good idea to have a bank account with money in it waiting for you when you move. You can arrange for your present bank to transfer your money and your safe deposit box contents to the new bank, if your bank has always been fast and efficient enough for you.

Otherwise, take the contents of your safe deposit box out of the bank and carry them with you as you move. Withdraw the money from your savings and checking accounts and carry it with you in traveler's checks or get a certified check for it. Put your money and safe deposit items in the new bank once you arrive in your new town.

• If you belong to a club with salable memberships, arrange to have yours sold for you. Find out if your present club has a relationship with another club in your new city—it can save a long wait.

• Find out if your move will be covered by your existing insurance policies. If not, try to arrange coverage. Find out if you can transfer your other insurance (fire and so forth) to your new home. This should be arranged to take effect as soon as you move.

• Arrange to have the utilities (gas, electricity, water) and telephone at your new home turned on and charged to you. Don't be surprised if you are asked for a substantial deposit even though you have a spotless payment record in your old home—this is becoming more and more customary.

In some cases, utilities can be turned on from outside

and, if there is a telephone in the house or apartment already, the telephone can be turned on from the business office.

If either or both of these cannot be done, arrange with a neighbor, the real estate agent, or a building superintendent to admit utility and telephone people.

● Arrange to have the utilities and telephone either turned off or transferred to the new occupants of your old house or apartment. Have the telephone remain in service through moving day so you can follow up on things as necessary.

● Let local merchants (liquor stores, record stores, dress shops, furniture stores, appliance stores) know that you are moving and need boxes. They'll save them for you if you take them away promptly. Find out when they want you to take away each group of boxes—every Tuesday? Tuesday and Thursday?—and be sure to do so. And don't forget to tell the stores when you have collected enough.

**AND NEXT . . .**

● Work out how the family will travel to the new home and when.

Will one person fly ahead while the rest drive? Will the entire family go by bus?

Arrange travel reservations if needed for transportation and for motel rooms along the way. You probably won't need motel reservations if you stop no later than four in the afternoon each day. Confirm any reservations that require confirmation.

● Plan family clothing for the trip and for the first five days in the new home in case the movers don't arrive. Put in some work clothes for the early stages of getting settled and one fairly dressy outfit for each family member in case someone in your new town invites you out for dinner.

A possible selection of clothes for women and girls would be:

        two pairs of jeans or other work pants
        one pair fairly dressy pants
        three T shirts
        one skirt
        one fairly dressy blouse or sweater
        sneakers
        sandals (summer)
        dressy shoes

and for men and boys:

        two pairs of jeans or other work pants
        one pair dressy slacks
        two T shirts
        one sport shirt
        one dressy shirt
        one tie
        one sports jacket
        sneakers
        sandals (if summer)
        dress shoes

In the winter, a lined raincoat can be very useful on this kind of trip. In the summer an unlined raincoat is equally useful. Both are not very bulky and can be rolled up. Remember to travel light.

• Work out how the family pets will be moved. They can go in the car, on the train (probably in the baggage car), or by air.

Take pets to the veterinarian for a health certificate

and (if necessary) a rabies shot. Have your pet's identification and rabies tag placed on his or her collar.

• Work out a plan for your plants, too. See Chapter 9, "Moving Plants and Pets."

• Be sure, if you will be driving a long distance, that your car is up to the trip. Have special attention given to the tires and brakes.

Be sure your car's tool kit isn't missing anything; if it is, replace it. In winter, be sure the car has snow tires or that there are chains in the back.

• Start packing, if you haven't already.

• It's not easy to move liquids without spilling. Throw out any liquids you have except for necessities.

Get rid of anything flammable. This means draining the oil and fuel from your power mower, throwing out cans of paint and oil, and getting rid of cleaning fluids.

• Have the rugs picked up if they are going to be cleaned and delivered to your new home.

• Return everything you've borrowed from libraries or neighbors over the years, and try to get back the things you've loaned. If you can't, forget it—they were probably good neighbors in other ways.

• If your appliances will need servicing, arrange to have this done as near as possible to the date of the move.

• Hold a garage sale or arrange for a charity to pick up things you are not taking with you—perhaps both.

• If possible, go out to dinner in a pleasant restaurant and relax.

## TWO OR THREE DAYS BEFORE

• Disconnect, empty, clean, and dry the refrigerator and freezer. Leave the doors open so they can dry thoroughly.

●If you want to, wash dirty clothes before the appliances are disconnected. If you don't want to, pack dirty clothes in their own box and label as dirty.

●Pack a small suitcase or box with things you may need if the van is delayed. Don't bother if your new home is half a block from a grocery store that's open 24 hours a day.

The following is a list of suggestions. Every family will have its own needs.

cake of soap
paper towels
cleanser
saucepan
coffeepot
coffee
paper plates
cups
forks, knives, and spoons
toilet paper
small first aid kit
peanut butter
jelly
crackers
bread (buy it on the road)
sugar
milk (buy it on the road)
tools, including hammer, pliers, screwdriver
flashlight
light bulbs

●Traveling and settling down to sleep will be easier if everyone packs a book or a magazine to read.

●All people who sleep with stuffed animals are in charge of transporting their own stuffed animals (with a little backing up by others). Don't pack stuffed animals in advance.

● You may want to pack some snacks to help the trip pass more pleasantly, but many people find that it's a good idea for everyone to stop now and then for a snack and a cold drink on a long journey.

● If no one has yet offered to look after your baby or toddler the day of the move, think about either asking someone to do so or hiring a sitter (an older child in the family might be fine).

## THE DAY BEFORE

● If the movers are packing for you, keep an eye on them. They may not like it, but you have the right to be sure the job is done properly.

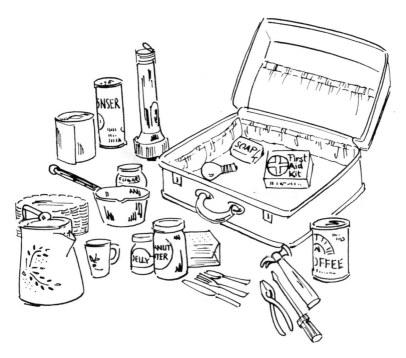

*If the van is delayed on a long distance move, a suitcase with things you may need is a good idea.*

With some movers, you'll realize within the first half hour that they care more about your things than you do and you can ignore them. Others will need constant supervision.

• If you are packing, don't pack the contents of bureau drawers—tape the drawers closed the day of the move and have them moved with their contents. Check to be sure they have nothing in them that will spill, leak, or break.

• Put your luggage and anything else you are taking with you in the car (if you are moving yourself by car), or move it all to one area of the house and put signs all over it saying "Don't Move," or lock it in a closet. Why? To avoid having it packed in something and then loaded on the van the next day.

• Label things you do not want moved "Do Not Load."

• Label things you want taken off the van first (your beds and bedding, for instance) with "Load Last."

• Unplug your television set or sets. This is to give them time to cool down—there's a remote chance they will crack if they are not cool.

## AND MOVING DAY . . .

• Don't be surprised if no one wants breakfast—moving is very exciting for everyone involved. If no one's hungry early, you can always get something to eat later in the day when you'll all enjoy it more.

• Have one person check your home from top to bottom to be sure everything is ready to go. Look in closets to be sure nothing is left hanging in the back. If your home is too big for one person to check, have different people do different floors.

• Somewhere (over the kitchen sink is a good place) leave your new address and telephone number (if you know it) so the next people to live in your old home can forward the mail that comes for you by mistake.

It's nice to add a list of useful names and addresses— a good butcher, the telephone numbers for fire and police—but not essential.

- Someone must be home on moving day to greet the movers, watch the movers, and lock up. If for any reason someone outside your family has to do this, give the moving company's agent the name and telephone number of this person. It's better, of course, to do the supervising yourself.

- Go with the mover as he or she tags everything with the moving company's numbers. Make sure everything you want moved, and nothing else, is marked.

- The driver will make an inventory of all your things, including a description of condition. Find out what the symbols mean if the driver uses symbols, and challenge any you disagree with, such as calling antiques "badly scarred" or exaggerating the poor condition of other items.

- You—or the person acting for you—must stay until everything is loaded. Check your home once again to be sure nothing has been missed before signing the inventory.

- Get your copy of the inventory from the driver. Keep it.

- Be sure the driver has the correct valuation on your items. See Chapter 8, "Working with the Movers."

- Be sure the driver has your new address. If you plan to camp out in your new home if the van is late, be sure the driver knows that. If you plan to stay somewhere else, be sure the driver knows the address and telephone number of the place where you can be reached. See Chapter 8, "Working with the Movers."

• Be sure everything (utilities and so forth) is shut off that you want off. Lock all the windows and doors. Leave the keys with someone in case of an emergency before the next tenant moves in.

• As you finally leave your old home you will suddenly be sure you forgot something.

Keep calm.

You probably didn't and if you did the new people will send it on to you.

• This chapter has only touched on moving with children. The next chapter discusses the entire area of helping children make a successful move.

## Don't Forget

There are so many big things to take care of during the course of a move that it's easy to forget about some of the things we normally take for granted.

We already mentioned that you should have some food around for your helpers if you are not using professional movers. Keep in mind that your family too deserves to eat and it is not a good idea to go off and leave the movers, however honest and efficient they are, alone. Many movers will, sensibly, refuse to work if there is no one home.

Don't try to cook the day of the move. Your food should all be given away or ready to go, your appliances should be packed up unless you are leaving them, and you have enough on your mind without planning meals for anyone and then washing dishes.

Instead, get some sandwiches from the delicatessen the day before or, if the weather is very hot and you have no refrigeration, the same day, and feed the family with those.

## COLD DRINKS, TOO

Have cold drinks around, too, including a pitcher of something like iced tea or lemonade and another of water. They should stay cool enough in a shady place if you don't have a refrigerator.

Get a lot of paper cups and establish some place to throw them away—you don't want to find a lot of used cups in your household furnishings when you arrive at your new home.

Put paper cups by the kitchen sink and by all the bathroom sinks, too, so that anyone, including the movers, can have a drink of cold water without having to ask for a glass.

## HEAT AND AIR CONDITIONING

Most of us are so accustomed to having heat in our houses that it's easy to walk out of a house and forget to turn it down. It will cost someone money if the heat is left on, and someone might very well be you. Turn the heat down (but not off) to about 50°. The reason for leaving it on is to prevent damage to the inside structure of the house and to keep water pipes from bursting.

In the summer, if there is air conditioning, be sure it is turned all the way off before you leave. There's no point in cooling a place when no one is there.

## UTILITIES

Since you notified the utility companies earlier, be sure they have either turned off the utilities or transferred the account to the next people moving in.

If they are supposed to be turned off the day you move, don't be shocked by how unhomelike your former home seems with no electricity to brighten it up.

Keep in mind that no electricity can mean problems

as far as water goes with certain kinds of pumps—if you have an electric pump, fill lots of pitchers with water for those involved in the move.

With all utilities, it's a common experience for people to move and later find that the utilities were never turned off. For that reason, it's probably a good idea to keep your phone working and have it turned off the day after the move. You'll also find it useful for tracking down the movers if they happen to be late and for making final arrangements of various kinds.

In any case, guard against the tendency we all have to be so used to things that we don't notice that the electricity and gas and water (if that's metered) are still on when they're supposed to be off.

## TIPPING THE MOVERS
It is generally considered the custom to tip professional movers. Truckers—whether amateur or professional— are delighted to accept tips, too.

How much you should tip isn't subject to any rules, but as a rough guide figure on about $5 per three hour stint per mover for a short, local move. Tip when the job is finished.

For the professional mover who is going away with all your worldly goods in a moving van, consider the tip as a method of ensuring at least a modicum of interest in your move. Tip each mover about $20 in advance— you may see everything sooner that way. And, yes, tip the same amount when your goods arrive in the new location.

## Organizing Your Move

The following chart is not meant to cover everything mentioned in this chapter, but rather to touch on some of the major points in organizing a move. Use the chart to nudge your memory, but follow it up by referring to the text.

**First**—Learn about your new city, find a home

**Next**—Decide how you will move, start working on change of address notices

**And Next**—Decide how the family will travel to the new home, start packing

**Two or Three Days Before Move**—Pack items for emergency use if the van is delayed, defrost refrigerator and freezer, wash last load of clothes

**Day Before**—If movers are packing, supervise them, put your luggage where it won't be loaded onto moving van

**Moving Day**—Supervise movers

# 5

# HELPING THE KIDS MAKE THE MOVE

Moving is difficult for adults but it can be even more difficult for children. Teenagers may tell you exactly what they think of the whole idea of the move ("It stinks") or try to be good mannered and polite about it while they feel miserable inside. Younger children may feel bewildered and lost as much at the thought of moving as at the reality, and it can be very difficult helping them, especially if you really don't want to move either.

These problems, of course, don't arise when a family is moving to a dream house that all the family has helped plan over a period of time. The fact remains, however, that there will be adjustments required and they can be difficult.

## Honesty

Plan from the beginning to be scrupulously honest with the children. Although many people say you should play up the positive side of a move and ignore the negative around children, most families experienced in moving say it's much better to present both sides of the story when there are two sides. You may even find the children comforting you, saying things like "You'll make new friends, Mommy and Daddy" if you're honest about your feelings.

Tell the kids as soon as you know that there will be a move. Tell them the exact date—or an approximate date if you don't know exactly—when the move will take place, rather than saying "Not for a long time" or "In the summer."

Make it clear that everyone in the family will be moving together. Children often have vague suspicions that they are going to be left behind. Make it clear to the children that all the family possessions will be moved, including ratty looking stuffed animals and puzzles

*As soon as you know it, tell your children the exact date of the move.*

with the pieces missing. Be sure the children know that their beds will be moved, too. Everyone likes to sleep in a familiar bed, and it means a great deal to most children.

## House Hunting

If you possibly can—and, of course, if you are moving nearby this is no problem—let the children take part in the house hunting. Obviously, they won't have the deciding vote, but they can help you make up your own mind and they will feel they are having a part in the process of choosing your new home.

Whether the children get to help choose the new home or not, be sure they see any photographs or sketches of it. Draw floor plans so they can have a chance at imagining it, including where their rooms are located. A child finds it very exciting to think that provision is being made for his or her room.

Find out as much as you can about the neighborhood so you can let the children know what it is like. Find out something about other children in the neighborhood (if the neighbors on either side have children the same age as your children you can stop worrying right away), how far the school is from your new home and how your kids will travel to get there.

## Moving Day

Moving day can be chaotic for everyone, including the children. If someone else is taking care of your children away from home make sure the children know when you'll be coming to get them so they don't start worrying that you've forgotten all about them.

If the children are going to be in the house, perhaps helping with the move, keep them away from the movers. This isn't because the children would do anything terrible, but because the movers may be rather irascible and any child is worried enough about moving without being snarled at.

If your child has a favorite stuffed animal to sleep with, be sure he or she packs it so it can be with him or her the minute it's needed. If your child is pretty good about not losing things, he or she may want to carry that stuffed animal the entire day of the move. Such an animal or a blanket or whatever can be a real comfort to a bewildered child.

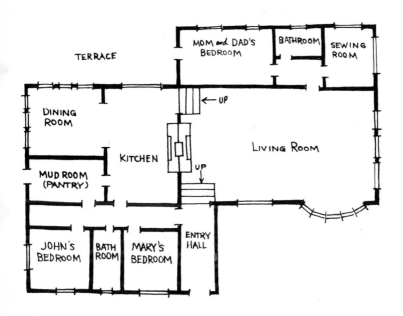

*A floor plan with their rooms labeled will help children to imagine what their new home is like.*

## Public School

Find out the name of the public school (even schools identified by numbers sometimes have names as well—they make a school a little more personal) and, if possible, the name of the principal and your child's teacher if it's an elementary school.

If there's anything special or different about the school your kids will be attending, tell them about that, too. This includes open classrooms, closed classrooms, prefabs, consolidated school districts, ungraded classrooms, carpeting in the hallways, swimming pools, tennis courts—you have the idea. Look for things that make the new school different from the one your children presently attend.

Explain to your children that the new school will have their records from the old school. Don't do this in a threatening fashion, but just matter-of-factly. Explain to your children that their records from the old school will probably be used for placement. Children who have had trouble of one kind or another in their old school may be afraid this will follow them to the new school. Actually, these records are very limited in what they say and most teachers prefer to make up their own minds about students.

How do you find your child's new school? Usually it's obvious—the nearest—but zoning of schools is sometimes a little peculiar so your best bet may be to call the local board of education.

If your new neighbors have children in school, they'll tell you the name and location of the school and give you information on how the children get there—whether they walk, take public transportation, or take a school bus.

If your children will be walking to school, tell them (and of course do it) that you'll walk to school with them either in advance or on the first day so they can learn the route.

If they'll go on public transportation, plan to go with them the first day—that can be somewhat frightening— and perhaps the first week. If there's a school bus, find out where it stops and walk with your kids to the stop.

In many neighborhoods, it's the custom for all the kids to walk to school together or take the school bus or public transportation together. If the neighborhood you're moving into is this kind of place, your child will be quickly absorbed into the community of children. In fact, an older child may offer to take your children for you the first day. An introduction to the group by a trusted older child is much better than being taken to school by your parent.

Find out how school closings for snow or inclement weather are announced. Is there a radio station that announces it? Does the firehouse whistle blow 10 times? Is there a round robin of telephone calls—and if so, is your family on it? This is important information to kids, as it holds out the promise of surprise school holidays.

# Non-Public School

Most public schools are pretty good and most kids in America go to public schools. You, however, for traditional family reasons, religious reasons, or because you've heard awful things about the public schools, may prefer a non-public school.

How do you find one? You find one the same way you

find clothes in a store—you shop. Check the public school at the same time you look for a non-public school to be sure you won't be paying for something that isn't quite as good. And for your children's sake, it's a good idea to find out where most of the neighborhood kids go to school. You can drastically limit the number of a child's friends by sending him or her to a school no one else in the neighborhood attends.

What do you look for in a non-public school? Well, one of the things these schools usually say they have going for them is that they transmit some form of philosophy. Be sure that this philosophy agrees with your own as much as possible. It's too hard on kids to come home from school glowing with some idea of how to live the good life only to be told by their parents, "That's nonsense!"

*Most children adjust easily to a new school.*

Look for academic excellence, if possible. If that's not possible, at least make sure the school is better academically than the public school.

How do you judge? Check college entrance records or entrance records for higher schools of one kind or another. Compare the curriculum offerings with those of other schools and check to be sure they are really offered and taught well. Some schools break up their courses into bits and pieces to add variety to the catalogue but don't really offer any in-depth variety.

Check the academic qualifications of the teachers on the staff. Be suspicious of a school that won't tell you about staff members' degrees and where they earned them.

If possible, try to talk to some children who go to the school—or better yet, because they're likely to get more honest answers, try to arrange for your kids to talk to kids who are students at the school.

Don't be bothered by reports of an eccentric teacher—every school is entitled to one eccentric—but if the feeling you get from the school is a very numb one, as if the kids are paralyzed by boredom, look for another school.

You may run into a situation where there isn't room in an independent school for your child for one reason or another, but it's less likely than it was a few years ago.

Above all, don't make getting into the particular non-public school a matter of life or death for your kids. If they don't get in because there isn't room or whatever, and end up in public school, you won't want them feeling themselves failures. Let them know the pros and cons of both the public and the non-public school and what the chances are for their admission to the non-public.

## Things to Do

What is there for kids to do in the new neighborhood? If
you haven't seen it, of course, it may be hard for you to
answer your children's questions, but if you know even
a little about it you may have some ideas.

If you're moving to a house in the suburbs and it's on
a dead end street, you can be pretty certain that the
neighborhood kids ride their bicycles and roller skate in
the street.

There may be a school playground nearby where
everyone in the neighborhood meets, or a town recreation field.

Perhaps there's a swim club (don't promise a swim
club, of course, if there's a long waiting list), or tennis
courts, or a big community playground where everyone
goes for cookouts and July 4th celebrations.

If you're moving to an apartment in the city, what do
the kids do to be near grass and get fresh air? Is there a
park they can go to? Are there beaches for summer
swimming or swimming pools?

Anyplace, no matter how apparently unprepossess-
ing, will have opportunities for kids to enjoy themselves, so if you don't know definitely say something
like "I don't know but I'm sure we'll find lots of things to
do once we get there."

If, for instance, you're moving to a house in the real
country, don't worry about the area not offering your
kids anything to do. The empty land around the town
will offer your kids lots of possibilities for good times.
And country towns often have very spirited community
celebrations for national holidays, as well as huge
dinners cooked by one of the churches or fraternal
organizations which the whole town goes to.

## MAKING FRIENDS

One of the advantages of having children in a family is that they do tend to force the adults to see what forms of fairly simple entertainment are available. You'll find that your children will lead you into situations you might never think of being in where you'll meet new people, some of whom will become good friends as time goes on.

Although it's important for you to tell your kids before the move the different things they'll be able to do, don't be surprised if they do none of the things you expect. Give them a push, if needed, to make friends and encourage them to bring friends home if possible, but don't try to dictate how they spend their free time. A child who likes to read a lot and considers walking to school more than enough exercise for a year is not likely

*A dead end street may be the neighborhood recreation center providing plenty of activities for your children.*

to want to go down to the schoolyard and shoot baskets all afternoon. You can encourage such a child to bend slightly in the direction of more activity, but it shouldn't be a matter of pressure and contention.

## Adjusting

Parents can do a lot to help a child's adjustment to the new neighborhood. You should probably try to spend a little more time with the kids when the move first takes place.

The little ones, especially, need to feel that the family is still the same, that home is still the same even though its physical surroundings have changed. Extra story time or a little more time talking together can make them feel at home again.

The older kids can be helped by parents, too. While most communities are friendly, some may be slower to warm up to newcomers than others.

If the children in your new area are cold or actively hostile, your children may find this terribly upsetting. Share with them your own feelings about new neighbors' coldness and try to reassure them.

## Be a Joiner

Help your children by joining various organizations. In this way you and your children will get to know other families like yours. This is true no matter where you may be living—city, suburb, or country.

The place to start, if you have a formal religion, is with your church or synagogue. In certain religions, you can ask your religious leader at the place you lived before for a "letter of transfer" and your new religious home will be expecting you Follow the practice of your own particular religion. This way your children will be able to start in some kind of religious school where they will meet other kids, and you will be able to meet other members. After that it's up to you how active or inactive you want to be. Don't decide at once—different branches of the same religion can be quite different depending on the leader and community.

As soon as you can, join the parents' organization at your children's school. At best, you can find this a chance to meet both parents and teachers; at worst, you won't meet the teachers but you will meet other parents who have children and are interested in schools.

If possible, agree to work on a few school projects. This will give you a direct pipeline to information about the school and the teachers in it, which can be very useful, and kids are usually proud to see their parents working at a cake sale or school supper. Furthermore, this is one way to get the point across to the school that you are a concerned parent—it's sad but true that schools often need that little extra motivation that comes from knowing of a parent's interest.

## High School Juniors

The basic assumption is, of course, that if the family is moving all the family is moving. Many people, however, confess themselves torn over what to do with a child who is nearing the end of junior year in high school, with all that implies about a last chance with high school friends and applications for college.

It's important not to make the mistake of figuring that because the child appears mature and independent there won't be any pain in the move. In fact, a child this old will often be more fearful of the move and see more of the negative aspects of it than a child who is younger.

Your high school junior deserves your time and your sympathetic understanding.

As far as the new high school is concerned, it's important for the staff to understand exactly what the child's hopes and plans are after graduation.

If you possibly can, visit the school before the move with your child to explain gently what a super kid he or she is and how much you want him or her not to lose anything by the move.

If you can't visit, a long distance telephone call to the principal (if it's a small school) or the head of guidance (if it's a large school) can be helpful. Whether you're making a visit or a telephone call, of course, don't come on too strong. Rather, present yourself as a member of a family looking forward to the experience of living in the new community and going to its wonderful schools, a family that wants to be sure that all members make the most of their time there, including the one who will be a senior.

Most kids adapt very well to a new school, even if it is in senior year. There are, however, a few kids who would really, for one reason or another, be better off in their old school—this is something that should be carefully considered. A student who will be the editor of the school paper or captain of an athletic team might want desperately to be allowed to stay in that school, especially if he or she has set sights on this goal for years. A student who has finally made friends after a difficult early adolescence, a student whose present school offers special courses or facilities that the new school cannot match, may also want to stay in the old neighborhood and the old school.

Can it be done? Sure, and it is done, all the time. Arrangements are made with a relative in town (probably the easiest and best arrangements to make), with the parents of a classmate, with someone living in the old neighborhood, or with a teacher for the student to live with them and visit parents for the longer vacations. Obviously, board is paid. This can be an interesting experience for all concerned.

Think about it from every angle—including how much you'll miss your child if he or she does live with some other family, and about how much your child will miss you. Be properly grateful to whatever family is taking your child in, but make clear to all that the arrangement is subject to change at any time.

# Looking at a School

The important thing about a school for most parents isn't whether it is public or independent, but whether or not the school feels right to the family and seems as if it will provide students with a sound education. You look, in other words, for all the elements that make up a "good" school. Here are some things to consider.

**Philosophy** (if independent)—Do you agree or disagree?

**Curriculum**—Are all subject areas covered, or are there gaps?

**Quality**—What is school's record for entrance to college?

**Faculty**—Do they seem enthusiastic and energetic, or are they bored stiff?

**Class Size**—If classes are large, are the teachers maintaining control; if small, is any teaching going on or is it more social?

**Physical Plant**—This is the least important aspect of a school but it's nice if there are enough desks for the students, if the walls and halls are fairly clean, and if the lighting is adequate. The age of the building doesn't matter provided it's well maintained.

# 6

# TAKING AND MAKING AN INVENTORY

Many people move without taking their own inventory; instead, they rely on the one prepared by the movers. Other people, however, consider their own inventory essential. An inventory can also be useful when you are not moving—for insurance purposes, for instance. You may never need it, but if you should have a fire someday, insurance companies seem to be more responsive if you do have an inventory.

This chapter will discuss ways to take an inventory. Each is satisfactory for moving as well as for other purposes for which the average family will need an inventory.

## The Room-by-Room Method

The first method, which we're calling "the room-by-room method," is probably the most usual, and it's the one for which the charts at the end of the chapter are designed.

Starting at one end of a room, work across to the other end, writing down the name and a brief description of each object in the room. For the living room you might write "armchair, blue" or, if you have two different blue armchairs in the room, "armchair, blue, mahogany arms" for one and "armchair, blue velvet" for the other. If you have two blue armchairs that are identical, of course, you would write "2 armchairs, blue."

The problem with taking a room-by-room inventory of your home is that it takes time. The more things you have, the more time it takes—and you may be short of time.

Inventories go much faster if there are two people working on the job. Have one person call out the items to be listed and the other person write them down. This way, each person can check the other. It's easy to miss something when you are working on your own.

At the same time that you list every item, put down the value of it. This can help you determine the valuation to declare to the moving company for your shipment and is worthwhile for other reasons. There is more on valuation below. See also Chapter 8, "Working with the Movers."

## WHAT TO LIST

Be sure to list everything. Include tablecloths, glasses, china, silverware, blankets, pillows, sheets, and towels.

Don't leave out records and tapes, typewriters, other business tools. The reason for mentioning this is not that we think you really would forget these things, but because many people who have made inventories have forgotten them—and then have had to add them after the fact.

Don't, in other words, list only your furniture and appliances. Even writing paper is worth listing if you've bought a huge supply—and if, of course, it will still be useable after the move.

As you make the inventory, list the date you bought each item. If you don't know (because you haven't kept the bills) or can't remember the date you bought something, make an educated guess. Most of us can remember within a year one way or the other when something was bought. Did you buy the sofa before you lost your job that time or after?

## VALUATION

The valuation of the items on your inventory is a somewhat sticky area. If the moving company loses, destroys, or just damages something, they may disagree strongly with your valuation of it.

However, you can often convince everyone involved if you have something to back up your valuation. For most items—the living room furniture, the kitchen appliances—the best thing to have is a bill showing what you paid. If you don't have the bill (many people just aren't bill keepers) you may have the cancelled check with which you paid for the item.

If you have neither the bill nor the cancelled check, you'll have to try to remember what you paid for it. This often seems to be surprisingly difficult, but do your best. The more people working on remembering, of course, the easier it should be.

A bill is not always the best way to handle valuation. For instance, you may have been given a good many pieces of furniture or rugs or whatever. You paid nothing for them but that doesn't mean they are valueless. Furthermore, some things—antiques, silverware—will become more valuable as time passes, unlike most of your household things which depreciate.

As far as the things you were given are concerned, your best bet is to value them at what they would have cost secondhand when you were given them.

Your antiques should not be valued at what they were worth when you bought them (you might have picked them up for a song), but at what their value is now—what it will cost to replace them.

It will probably be fairly easy to judge the value of your silverware now. Don't guess—simply go to a store that sells your pattern and find out what it costs.

It's important to keep in mind when you value these items that you are valuing them in a different way from the other items. Mark clearly on your inventory that for silver and other things that appreciate, you are listing "today's price" rather than what you paid initially. If by

*The room-by-room method of taking inventory goes faster if two people work on the job. One can call out the items to be listed while the other writes them down.*

any unfortunate chance you lost one of these appreciated items, you would certainly not want to be given a percentage of the cost to replace it as you would for items that depreciate with time.

With any kind of valuation, of course, it's important that you stick up for your rights if a question comes up concerning the value of a lost or damaged item. At the same time, it would be a mistake to ignore the fact that all of us become so attached to the things in our homes that we tend to ignore their failings—the stuffing coming out of the arm of the chair, the gouge out of the dining room table, even that film of gray dirt that gradually covers upholstered furniture.

## Inventory as You Pack

The second method of making an inventory is to make it as you pack. This presumes, of course, that you will be doing the packing yourself.

While some people have inventoried their possessions successfully as an integral part of packing, others have found they simply ran out of both time and inclination to do this.

This method does, however, have the virtue that you get two jobs finished at once, and your possessions will be inventoried according to the way in which they were packed rather than according to the way they were placed in your old home.

For this inventory, use a pad of lined paper with a sheet of carbon paper. Use a ballpoint pen to make your inventory—it will get through to the carbon better for the copy. In making two copies, you will also be making a packing list for the outside of boxes or whatever.

If you are packing dishes, for instance, wrap one

group of the same size (dinner plates, perhaps), then put them in the carton in which they are being moved and write down the number and a description ("china" or "earthenware") with as much additional information as you need to describe them fully. Once the entire carton has been packed, attach the carbon of your inventory list to the outside of the carton. Use cellophane tape and tape all over the list—not just around the outside edges—to keep it from being ripped off accidentally in the moving.

How do you inventory something like a sofa with this system? You certainly want to have a record of it, but you can hardly go around sticking sheets of paper to it or to such things as Great Aunt Bella's corner cabinet.

Actually, if you can get to the back of the corner

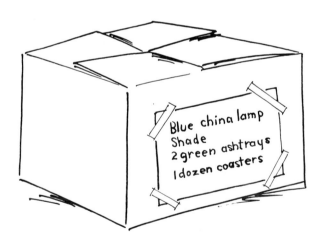

Blue china lamp
Shade
2 green ashtrays
I dozen coasters

*The inventory-as-you-pack method creates a packing list for the outside of the box.*

cabinet (the part that will be against the wall, now and forever) or to the bottom of the sofa, you may find a wooden section to which the inventory paper can be attached without ruining the furniture. But if you can't find such a place, or feel pulling cabinets away from the wall and turning sofas upside down is more than you want to do, use the room-by-room (in this case piece-by-piece) inventory method and list these pieces without making a carbon to attach to them.

To work out the value of the items in an inventory made this way, follow the same steps as listed in the valuation section (above). Add up the value of the individual items in cartons for a total value.

## The Photographic Method

One of the easiest ways to take and make an inventory is with a camera. At one time, insurance companies frowned on photographic inventories, but these are now acceptable. They should be accompanied by some additional information—notably value.

If you have some very valuable antique furniture, photographs can be especially helpful if it disappears— which we certainly hope won't happen.

The best way to take a photographic inventory is room by room. In the case of valuable antique furniture, take pictures from several angles but make clear the pictures are of the same piece of furniture. If you have two antiques that look the same, photograph them together.

A photographic inventory, of course, can't wait until the last minute. You will have to get the pictures back from the developer and then indicate on each one the value and, if it is relevant, the date you purchased the item.

Don't photograph books, records, china, or silverware individually, unless you want to highlight a particularly valuable item. You'd never be finished and you'd spend the rest .of your life working to pay for the film you used. Instead, photograph a wall of books, a cabinet of records, a pile of china to indicate the quantity you have.

You can use color film to confirm a special coloring (in an eighteenth-century piece of Delft, for instance), but take most of your pictures in black and white. Colored prints have a tendency to change color over a period of years, and although film manufacturers believe they have solved this problem, it's just as well to be safe. A color picture that has changed color can give a false impression.

*The photographic method is one of the easiest ways to take inventory.*

Keep the photographs in an album—the kind with plastic pages you slip the pictures into is ideal. Write all the valuation information either in the front of the album (and remember to put the date on which you made the valuation) or on the back of the pictures themselves.

## Exception Inventory

An exception inventory—as its name suggests—isn't really a complete inventory, but it can be useful. This is an inventory only of the exceptional items—things of great value, whether sentimental or monetary, or things you believe might prove tempting to others, such as large quantities of liquor (although you might do better to get rid of this with a series of parties before moving).

Under this system, you don't inventory the sofa or the old shag rug in the bedroom, but you do inventory the oriental rug. You don't inventory the bulk of the record collection, but you would inventory your original Bessie Smiths on the Grey Gull label. You don't inventory your costume jewelry, but you do inventory great-grandmother's diamond ring, even if the diamond has a slightly yellow cast.

The theory behind this method of inventory is that in the case of these valuables replacement will be both expensive and difficult. Be sure that you don't overlook any of them and that you have valued them in advance.

### PROFESSIONAL APPRAISAL

The question of the valuation of items leads naturally to the question of whether or not you should have certain items appraised by a professional. If you have some extremely valuable items, such as near-priceless paintings, your insurance company will probably insist that you have them appraised and have them reappraised every so often to reflect an increase in value.

If, on the other hand, you have some items—family jewelry, perhaps—that you would like to have appraised just to find out what they are worth now, remember that this can be an expensive proposition for relatively little return.

Consider great-grandmother's diamond ring, for instance, last appraised in the 1920's when, as far as anyone can remember since no one wrote it down, the value was given at $800. Now, since the value of diamonds (even ones with a yellow cast) is moving upward rapidly, it may be worth $2000, perhaps even more. Now that you're moving, is it worthwhile having it appraised just to find out if it has appreciated this much?

Most appraisers charge 10% of the appraised valuation for an appraisal. The charge percentage usually goes down as the valuation goes up, and is also affected by whether or not the appraisal is formal (with a written statement) or informal (just a verbal evaluation).

If it's worth it to you, or if you feel certain items need to be reappraised so you can increase your insurance coverage, go ahead. But keep in mind that if great-grandmother's ring is now valued at $2000 it will probably cost you $200 to find out, and you can buy a lot of things for your move with $200 that you might enjoy more.

## The Movers' Inventory

As we said earlier it is perfectly possible to move without your own inventory. If you do or if you don't, you must still pay a great deal of attention to the inventory the movers will make.

The driver of the van will have his own inventory list. Be certain it agrees with your list or have someone stick to the driver like glue as it is made. Be sure that you agree with notations concerning the condition of your items.

The notation is made with initials. Don't guess at what the initials mean—ask. If you disagree strongly with the condition of an item as noted and the driver refuses to change his listing of the condition, indicate on both copies of the driver's inventory that you disagree and what you feel the actual condition to be.

Be sure you get a copy of the movers' inventory. Keep this, of course, until you are finally moved and everything is settled to your satisfaction.

For further discussion of valuing your goods for the move, see Chapter 8, "Working with the Movers."

# Charts for Room-by-Room Inventory

| Room | Number if More Than One | Year Bought | Cost | Today's Value |
|------|-------------------------|-------------|------|---------------|
| Living Room | | | | |
| Dining Room | | | | |
| Family Room | | | | |

| Room | Number if More Than One | Year Bought | Cost | Today's Value |
|------|-------------------------|-------------|------|---------------|
| Den | | | | |
| | | | | |
| Study/ Library | | | | |
| | | | | |
| Playroom | | | | |

| Room | Number if More Than One | Year Bought | Cost | Today's Value |
|---|---|---|---|---|
| Bar |  |  |  |  |
| Kitchen |  |  |  |  |
| Breakfast Room |  |  |  |  |

| Room | Number if More Than One | Year Bought | Cost | Today's Value |
|------|-------------------------|-------------|------|---------------|
| Pantry | | | | |
| Patio | | | | |
| Halls | | | | |

| Room | Number if More Than One | Year Bought | Cost | Today's Value |
|------|-------------------------|-------------|------|---------------|

Bedrooms

| Room | Number if More Than One | Year Bought | Cost | Today's Value |
|------|-------------------------|-------------|------|---------------|
| Bathrooms | | | | |
| | | | | |
| Attic | | | | |

| Room | Number if More Than One | Year Bought | Cost | Today's Value |
|------|-------------------------|-------------|------|---------------|
| Basement | | | | |
| Utility Room | | | | |

| Room | Number if More Than One | Year Bought | Cost | Today's Value |
|------|-------------------------|-------------|------|---------------|
| Yard |                         |             |      |               |
|      |                         |             |      |               |
| Garage |                       |             |      |               |

# 7

# MOVING YOURSELF AND YOUR FAMILY

Getting your household goods packed and on their way to your new home is only part of the battle. Unless you're moving a very short distance, you still have to move yourself and your family.

## What You Take

Before you start packing the things you'll take with you, or planning what they'll be, it's a good idea to remember certain basics.

Start by facing the fact that no matter how hard you try, you'll end up with more leftover things than you expect.

Tell your family well ahead of time that things to be taken with you are strictly limited to the contents of one suitcase, one shopping bag, or one box per person. This will probably prove impossible to stick to, but it's a beginning.

If you're going by car, avoid the temptation (it hits everyone in the throes of packing) to say, "We'll take it in the car." You'll have plenty of things that really must go in the car even if you do try as hard as you can to limit everyone to one bag or box.

## Other Ways to Go

Not everyone, of course, will travel by car. If you don't, it is a good idea to limit your luggage even more.

If, of course, you plan to do most of your moving by air, as discussed in Chapter 2, "Choosing How to Move," you'll probably have more luggage than anyone else on the flight—the important point is that anything you take with you should be taken for a solid, valid reason, rather than just because it was left over.

If you are traveling a great distance (from one end of the country to the other) and don't have a lot of time, flying may be the best answer for the entire family. It has the advantages that your pet can travel with you (in the hold—don't worry, it's pressurized too), and it's quick.

If you're worried about what it will cost to fly rather than drive or take a bus, try to figure in what you'll be saving on meals and beds.

One of the disadvantages of flying to your new home is that you will arrive well before the moving van— even if it comes quickly, directly, and right on time. Maybe you can arrange to take a vacation in your new part of the country so the whole family can get to know it, or maybe you can visit relatives for a while before flying to your new home. Otherwise, alas, you'll be faced with lodging and food bills until the van arrives, unless you can get early access to your new home and don't mind camping out. More on that in Chapter 8, "Working with the Movers."

Train travel is one way to get around the problem of arriving far in advance of the van. A long train trip can be very enjoyable, especially if your route takes you through new parts of the country.

Train travel lends itself to lots of baggage even less than car or plane travel. If you are going on a really long train journey, it is best to insist that people limit their baggage to one suitcase.

Your pet? What happens to pets seems to vary from train to train. Check with the railroad. In some cases, your pet can travel with you, and the train personnel may even offer to take your pet for walks at the long stops. Or, your pet may live in the baggage car, be spoiled by the baggage car attendant, and have a ball. In some cases, you can bring your pet if he or she is in a carrying case. And in other cases you won't be permitted to bring your pet at all. In such a case, consider sending your pet by air.

Buses criss-cross the United States, going to small and large towns alike.

*If you are moving a great distance consider traveling to your new home by train, bus, or plane.*

Bus travel usually costs less than either air travel or train travel and, because buses tend to stop for meals at fairly modest places, you may save on food, too.

The disadvantage of bus travel is that, even in the most comfortable of buses, the seats tend to grow uncomfortable as the hours pass. In a train and, to a limited extent, on a plane, you can get up and walk around when you get stiff. With a bus, although limited movement is possible, there simply isn't the same chance to exercise. Keep that in mind when planning how to travel.

Buses, like trains, have relatively limited space for luggage. To be safe, don't count on taking more than two suitcases, or a suitcase and a duffle bag. There is very little room at the seats of most buses for luggage, so if you plan to keep some at your seat be prepared for a cramped, uncomfortable trip.

## Traveling by Car

Most people, however, will travel to their new home by car. One reason is that it may well prove to be the cheapest way of getting there; another reason is that the car, if you own one, will have to be moved one way or another, and you might as well do it. (If you do decide to ship it, the moving company can arrange for it to go either in a moving van or on a car trailer. If you prefer, you can use a company that specializes in driving cars from one end of the country to the other.)

Take with you in the car anything you are especially concerned about, which would include anything breakable and of real value to you, anything of extraordinary value, such as real jewelry, and anything irreplaceable, such as old photographs.

If you love plants, you may also have plants in the car. They'll travel best if they are packed in a box with newspaper between each plant and the box is held on someone's lap. If you love animals (plants and pets are not, of course, mutually exclusive), you'll probably have your pet in the car, too.

You may want to let your pet sit on the seat like everyone else and look out the window, but in the long run it may be best to move your pet in a carrier. You can get them through kennels, the ASPCA, from pet stores, or from a veterinarian.

If you have never taken your pet on a long journey by automobile, it might be a good idea to ask your veterinarian whether he or she recommends some kind of drug to keep your pet relaxed. This is also true if your pet travels by plane. See also Chapter 9, "Moving Plants and Pets."

*Traveling by car enables you to take any possessions you are particularly concerned about—breakable items, plants, pets.*

The biggest question is how far you are traveling. This will help you decide whether a few family members should drive while others fly, for instance, and how much can be taken in your car. The longer the distance, the more you should try to eliminate from being carried in the car.

## Enjoying the Trip

Even though you are driving for a purpose, there's no reason why the trip can't be pleasant. If one member of the family has to be in your new city before the others, it's probably better to have that person fly than to rush the trip for everyone else.

Earlier, we mentioned that motel reservations might be necessary if you planned to stop driving fairly late. If you stop around four o'clock, you should have no trouble finding a motel with space. Furthermore, stopping at four gives you a chance to wash up before dinner and unwind from the driving.

If you're a camping family and the weather is suitable, why not make your trip to your new home a camping trip as well as travel? This can save you a bundle of money. Of course, if you plan to do this, your camping equipment must go in the car—giving you an added reason for not taking too many other things in the car. There are more and more campgrounds all across the country and some good guides to them. Check your library and bookstore, and look into American Youth Hostels.

Don't start driving at the crack of dawn and keep going all day without a break. Many experienced travelers recommend stopping once in the morning and once in the afternoon for a hot or cold drink of some kind. It seems to revive everyone and improve dispositions.

Take an hour for lunch. This is especially important if one person is doing all the driving.

You don't have to spend a lot of money for lunch, and you probably won't want to since you'll be eating in restaurants so much on your trip. You can buy bread, sliced meat and cheese or various spreads, and make sandwiches for lunch. If the weather's cold, you'll have to eat your picnic lunch in the car, but if the weather is warmer, find a spot you like and picnic there. In any case, be sure everyone making the trip has a chance to walk around.

We've assumed that you'll be staying in motels on the journey if you're not camping out, but there are other options.

In some families, relatives are more than happy to help each other out by offering beds and breakfasts to all family members; in others, while relatives are glad to know you're passing through, they'd never dream of asking you to stay. You know your own relatives best. Of course, if you do hope to stay with at least a few relatives and friends as you move across the country, you'll make these arrangements far in advance—and offer them hospitality in your new city.

Some parts of the country have tourist homes, which are almost always less expensive than motels and usually very pleasant. Look for them off the highway—they're usually on the main street of a town.

You may also find it's worth the time to go off the highway for breakfast and dinner. The average coffee shop in a town is less expensive than the average motel restaurant. Sometimes the food is better, too. It's worth trying now and then.

## Moving a Baby

A baby usually requires a lot more equipment than an older child, including such things as diapers (disposable diapers are really the only answer if you're driving a long distance to your new home), baby food, and fairly frequent bottles.

You'll probably find your baby a good traveler most of the time. Most little ones like the motion of a car and seem to enjoy the scenery passing by them.

Food will be surprisingly little trouble, too. If your baby isn't yet eating solid foods, take along a couple of jars of baby food and plan to use it up at breakfast and lunch or lunch and dinner. Don't try to keep an opened jar of baby food overnight. Baby food should be refrigerated, and even if it's cold weather when you're traveling you shouldn't take a chance by keeping an opened jar too long.

If your baby drinks a lot of milk you can buy a quart every day, throwing out what's left over. It may be easier to ask restaurants to fill the bottle with milk or, easiest of all, take one of the powdered milk baby formulas with you and mix the milk as you need it. That way you'll have no need to worry over the milk souring.

While your baby may be an angel as long as the car is moving, it may be a different story when you stop for the night—you may find your baby crying like mad. Try to guard against this as much as possible by stopping fairly early (babies seem to get overstimulated by being awake past their bedtimes) and by taking a certain amount of your baby's environment with you.

If your baby is very little, you may have a carry bassinet that can be used for all occasions. If your baby is older, you can't travel with the well-loved crib but you can travel with the crib bumper (which makes up most of what a baby sees) to make a motel's crib seem more like home. A collapsible carriage that your baby is willing to sleep in may not only solve your travel problems but also be a real boon if the moving van is late arriving at your new home.

No matter what you do, you may find your baby crying when he or she is put to bed. Your impulse will be to pick up the baby, but you may have better luck by letting the tears continue for as long as half an hour. This will give the baby time to get a lot of excess feelings out and go to sleep. If the baby cries beyond half an hour, pick it up, soothe it, and sit with your baby quietly for a while before trying again.

*If you are moving a great distance consider staying overnight at tourist homes—they are usually pleasant and less expensive than motels.*

## Older Children

Traveling a long distance to a new home with older children won't necessarily be better or worse than traveling with a baby, but it will be different.

Probably you'll find that the older the child, the better the traveler. Very young children have little concept of either time or distance, no matter how hard you work at explaining terms such as "moving," "new house," "far away," and "six days."

One parent was thrown into despair when, after three days on a train traveling to a new home in a new state, the family's three-year-old said, "All right, Mommy. Let's get a taxi and go home." In a case like that, the only thing to do is go into the whole long story again and hope eventually the child will begin to understand it.

Children a little older than that have a better idea of time and distance, but not much. This is the group that has a favorite question, "Are we there yet?"

This is a good time, unfortunately, to introduce some form of entertainment. We say unfortunately because while the younger set tends to rejoice in many of the car games, they can be a little tedious for the adults. Everyone knows them, or knows some of them. You can collect license plates, for instance, giving points to the person who sees and identifies a license plate first, with the largest number of points for the plate from the most distant state. You can count animals, with a point system based on so many for a cow, so many for a horse, and a huge quantity for, say, a mountain lion.

## Don't Forget to Pay

You'll need money to pay for meals in restaurants, food you buy in grocery stores, and gasoline and other items for the car, to say nothing of rooms for the night.

Take enough money to be sure you're not going to run out on the road—and don't count on cashing a personal check if you do have a cash shortage.

Don't make the mistake of counting up the money you have to pay the movers if the cost of the move is over the estimate and deciding you can spend it to travel. Keep that intact somewhere.

Figure high for your daily expenses when traveling. Any money left over can always be used.

Take some money in cash to start with, the rest in traveler's checks. Pay with traveler's checks when you can—most motels, for instance, will accept them without any question. Meals, gas, and incidentals will probably have to be paid for in cash.

If and when you need more cash go to a bank with your traveler's checks. You'll probably have to go into a town to find a bank—main highways usually don't have them.

And try as you travel to make the trip to your new home something of an adventure for the entire family.

# Ways to Travel

| Method | Advantages | Disadvantages |
|--------|-----------|---------------|
| Car | Car is moved; family, pets, plants are together; family owns car | Time involved; expenses for food and shelter while traveling |
| Bus | Low cost; buses go to many small towns; possibly more luggage can be carried than in car | Tedium and discomfort of long journeys (lack of room to walk around); excess time taken because of routing and stops |
| Train | Pleasant views; chance to walk around and avoid stiffness | Time involved (compared to plane); many stations have been closed in recent years |
| Plane | Speed (no other method comes close); possibility of taking many pieces of luggage (at a price) | Discomfort of seating (much less comfortable than bus, but trip usually shorter); direct flights only between larger cities |

# 8

# WORKING WITH
# THE MOVERS

Knowing what you can expect from professional movers, what your rights are in relation to them, and what to do if any problems come up can make moving much more pleasant. In this chapter, we will detail, step by step, how to go about making a better move with professionals.

## Estimates First

Once you know you are going to move, call at least three moving companies (unless there's one that several of your friends can recommend without qualification) and ask each one for an estimate.

Be sure the estimator goes through your entire house (not just one or two rooms) and really looks at everything you plan to move. An estimate based on anything less than a thorough check of your possessions is worthless.

Go with the estimator during this tour in order to point out items you don't plan to take with you. Ask the estimator for information on packing so you can decide whether or not you want to have the moving company pack for you. Tell the estimator the date you plan to move and the location of your new home.

The estimate, as the moving companies will point out to you repeatedly, is not necessarily the final cost. For this reason, don't give your business to the company that comes in with the lowest estimate—they may be in the habit of giving low estimates to get business from people who don't realize an estimate isn't a firm price. Be suspicious, in other words, of any price that is a great deal lower than the other prices you are given.

The purpose of getting three estimates isn't to help you save money. Moving companies charge almost or exactly the same. You use the three estimates instead to try to get some feeling for the company you'll be working with in your move.

If the estimator gives you the impression of being

*Get estimates from at least three moving companies before deciding on the one you will use.*

honest, if you get a high estimate when others are low (which often turns out to be more accurate), or the estimator gives you some sound advice on how you can keep costs down, that's an indication that at your starting point at least, this company may be pretty good.

## When to Move

Most people don't have a choice about when to move. They move when the lease is up, or when the new job starts. If you do have a choice of when to move, you'd think there would be a best time of the year, wouldn't you?

Well, there is and there isn't, or at least that's the case if there are children involved. Most people who know something about kids, or remember their own childhoods, feel that, ideally, moves would be made at the end of the school year. That way, the new home and the new grade and the new school with the new classmates would all come more or less at the same time.

The problem with moving in summer is that this is the busiest time of the year for movers—many other people want their children to finish out the school year.

It would be one thing if the movers were just busy in summer. Unfortunately, because they are so busy, movers also perform more poorly during the summer months than at any other time of year. This means the movers are more likely to be late picking up your household goods and delivering them during this time.

The other busy times for movers are at the end of the month and the beginning of the month—every month—when homes tend to change hands. Movers don't work on weekends or holidays, either, so you can forget about that possibility.

Although the following appraisal isn't really accurate, it can perhaps give you some idea of the difficulties involved in picking out a "good time" to move.

• Start with the assumption that there are 51 "mover weeks" in the year—the one week that has been deducted is deducted for five holidays. With a five-day week, that's 255 days.

• Deduct five days per month for the busy times at the beginning and end of the month. That gives you 195 days.

• The summer months are "not good" for moving, so deduct 15 five-day weeks for a little of May, all of June, July, and August, and part of September. That leaves you with 120 days for the entire year which, we can assume, will be better than the rest.

• Divide this by 12 (the number of months in the year) and you only have 10 days a month for the movers to do a good job. Actually, that was cheating a little because the summer months are out of the picture. However, even if you figure about 8½ months (12 months minus the summer months) there are only 14 days left.

The calculations above aren't really meant to be taken entirely seriously, but they do indicate a situation that may suggest why it is difficult to pick a good time to move and why, even if you do pick a good time theoretically, it may not be a good time in practice.

How do you choose a time to move, then?

• If you have no choice of when to move, move when you must. If it's outside the busy summer season you may have the bonus of a "better" move.

• If for one reason or another you must move during the busiest times, go ahead and do it rather than making complicated arrangements to move into a hotel.

• If you feel it is extremely important to both move

during the busiest time and to have your household goods at your new home the day you and your family arrive, consider having the van pick up several days before you must leave your old home and camping out for the remainder of the time. One family member should then go ahead to meet the van at the new location.

The truth of the matter, however, is that there is no really "good" time to move—too many elements can cause a delay of one kind or another. It might be a comfort to know that one of the best moves we've heard of in researching this book was made in February, from a snowstorm in upstate New York to a snowstorm in upper Vermont.

## Movers' Liability

There is a standard liability, which movers are required to pay, for loss or damage. This is included in what you pay the movers for moving you—but it isn't adequate.

The standard liability is 60¢ per pound. This means you might have something valued at $250, but if it weighed only six pounds, you'd only receive $3.60 if it were lost. The standard liability, in other words, is simply not sufficient. If for some reason you want to accept this liability, you write "60¢ per pound per article" on the Bill of Lading.

Instead of taking the standard liability, there are two things you can do. By not writing anything on the Bill of Lading, the movers' liability becomes $1.25 for each pound of the total weight of the shipment, not per article. The liability, in other words, for one valuable item in a 5,000 pound load could go as high as $6,250—not likely, but theoretically possible.

If you feel this still might not result in a high enough amount if anything happened, list each item with value minus (in depreciated items) depreciation.

Both of these types of liability coverage will cost you 50¢ for each $100 of value. Don't try to save money here—this coverage is definitely worth having. For one thing, movers do not take (and are not required to take) responsibility for breakable items you pack yourself— your dishes and glasses, for instance—unless you have the 50¢ for each $100 of value type of coverage. For how to claim on this liability coverage, see the section on claims (page 149).

## The Cost of the Move

The cost of the move is figured by the total weight of the load the van carries and the distance to be traveled. Various other charges may be thrown in, including charges for packing and for your liability coverage.

The weight must be figured minus the weight of the van, and no one is supposed to be on the van except the driver. Weighing can be watched by you or your agent and must take place on scales certified by your local or county weights bureau. If you don't go to the scales with the truck, ask to see the driver's manifest when your goods are finally delivered so you can be sure the weight of the truck was subtracted. If you don't believe the weight of the load, do something about it before the movers start to unload the van at your new home.

Keep in mind certain points. First of all, most household appliances, chests of drawers, and so forth are extremely heavy. Books and records, in groups, weigh a tremendous amount. It is quite likely that the movers' weight will prove to be correct.

If the weight seems completely out of line to you, you have the right to demand that the van be reweighed in your presence. If you are right, the movers pay for this reweighing—if you are wrong, and the movers had the weight correct, you will pay for it. The movers' original weight is considered wrong (and they must pay) if it is more than 120 pounds over the reweighed weight or more than 25% over the weight on the estimate.

Earlier in this book we discussed packing and the pros and cons of having the movers do it for you. Packing is one of the "extras" that can build up a moving bill, since it is figured with a charge for the box itself plus a charge for the labor, which varies from city to city. For more information, see Chapter 3, "Starting to Pack."

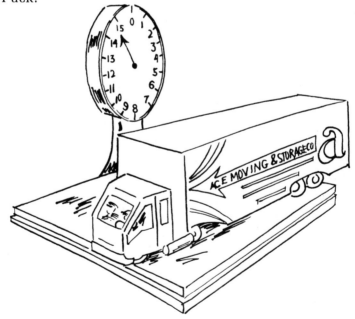

*The cost on the move is based on the total weight of the load the van carries and the distance to be traveled.*

The basic charge for moving includes carrying your household goods from your home to the van—but only a certain distance. If you live in an apartment house, for instance, be prepared for a hefty extra charge for the distance from the door of your apartment to the loading dock or street.

In addition, movers have other charges. Using an elevator in the apartment building, for instance, will often mean an extra charge of around 75¢ for every 100 pounds. If they have to climb stairs to get to your house or apartment, the cost is something like 35¢ to 50¢ per flight (and probably grumbling movers). That piano you're so proud of can be a problem, too (if it will go in through the door and doesn't have to be brought in or out through the window—a whole other game). Movers charge $20 to $30 for these, depending on size, and of course, there's an additional charge for stairs and elevators.

All this should be made abundantly clear by the person who estimates the cost of your move, but possibly will not be. For your part, to be sure the estimate will be as accurate as possible, call the attention of the estimator to stairs, elevators, long walks, and pianos in your present home. In addition, and very importantly, tell the estimator about any great distances, elevators, or stairs in your new home. This is to be sure the movers won't be met by any unpleasant surprises at either end—and so they can't say they didn't know about these things.

## The Paper Work

Working with movers will find you excessively involved in various forms of paper work. The first will be the estimate. There's no point in keeping the estimates from movers you decide not to use, but do keep the one from the movers you decide to use.

Once you have picked the mover you will use arrange with the agent to sign the Order for Service. This is when the agent will agree on the date for your household goods to be picked up at your old home and delivered to your new home. You will probably, as we mentioned earlier, have to agree on a span of days, but despite this precaution the movers may still be late. Take this into account when you are discussing pickup timing with the agent, and schedule the last day of the span of days well before you must leave your old home.

Some moving companies have an arrangement called "Expedited Service," which simply gives you a half-promise that your shipment will be delivered on a definite date. There's a charge for this (of course) if the

*An additional fee of 75¢ per 100 pounds may be charged if an elevator must be used in moving.*

movers actually make that date—which doesn't always happen. The charge varies according to the total cost of your shipment. It's worth discussing with the agent.

The next piece of paper that will confront you when you are moving is the driver's inventory. We discussed this earlier. Go with the driver as he tags items to be moved and puts on his inventory list the condition of each item. Be sure you agree with him about the condition of each item before signing the inventory. If you can't persuade the driver to change the listing of condition, write on both the driver's copy and your copy of the inventory that you disagree before you sign.

Keep your copy of the inventory. You will need it when the van is being unloaded at your new home.

The next thing to come up will be the combination Bill of Lading and Freight Bill. This is the form on which you will put the declared valuation of your shipment.

The Bill of Lading is a fairly standard form that explains the conditions under which the mover moves your household goods. As in the case of most such documents, this one is designed primarily to protect the mover, not you. There is almost no chance whatsoever of your persuading the movers, and certainly not the driver, to change any part of the Bill of Lading, so don't spend a lot of time over it. Insert your valuation information and sign it, being sure that the name of the agent at your destination is shown.

## Keeping Track

After the movers' van has driven away with all your worldly goods is not the time to suddenly wonder how you would ever find it if it disappeared (although you could probably get the information from the local agent).

Instead, get the following information before the van leaves:

- the name, address, and telephone number of the agent at your destination
  - the name of the driver of your van
  - the number of the shipment
  - the route the van will take to your new home

Don't be surprised if the van's route seems less direct than it might. Most vans travel with more than one shipment of household goods on them. This is one of those facts of moving life you can't do much about. Although well-meaning friends may advise you to insist that your goods travel alone, you are unlikely to have this happen on the average move, and if you said grandly "And charge me for it," the price would be prohibitive.

*If the movers have to climb stairs to get to your house or apartment, there may be an additional charge of 35¢ to 50¢ per flight.*

Be sure the driver of the van has the exact and correct address of your new home.

Be sure the driver knows an address and a telephone number for you if you are not going directly to your new home. It's a good idea to give the same information to the local agent.

If you are going to your new home, be sure the driver and agent know this, too.

Once you arrive in your new city, let the agent know at once that you are there—even if you arrive well in advance of the expected arrival of the van. Vans do, on occasion, arrive ahead of the scheduled date.

Once you get to your destination and have notified the agent of your arrival, stay there. The driver of the van will (or is supposed to) notify the agent 24 hours before he expects to arrive with the van. The 24 hours supposedly will give the agent enough time to notify you that your shipment is on the way. This 24-hour period includes only eight business hours during which you are likely to be notified unless the agent is extremely conscientious.

For this reason, and so you won't feel yourself permanently tied to the place where you've said you can be reached, it's a good idea to call the agent once a day after you first report in—whether or not it makes you popular with the agent. This way you can even go away overnight, provided you call to ask if there's any news on your shipment.

In any case, if your shipment is delayed past its scheduled arrival, the agent is required to let you know where your household goods are and in what condition (if, for instance, something really dreadful happened to the van).

If they arrive ahead of time, the driver can deliver your goods—but only with your permission. If for one reason or another you do not give permission (you haven't arrived yet, or your new home still has people living in it) the moving company can store your goods at their expense. Storage is not the best solution to any problem connected with moving (more things seem to get damaged in storage than during any other part of the usual move), so if it's at all possible, try to arrange to accept delivery.

## The Unloading

Whether or not the agent has notified you (another reason for keeping in touch), 24 hours after the driver has notified the agent that he's almost there the van will pull up at the address given as your new home. If for one reason or another there is no one there to meet it, the van will wait one hour if it has come more than 100 miles but less than 200 miles, and three hours if it has come more than 200 miles. After that, the driver will drive away and put your household goods in storage, at your expense.

If for some reason you are delayed on the road to your home, authorize someone else to meet the van and tell the agent this person's name and telephone number. The best person to be selected for this—because of the problem of getting a key to anyone else (unless you were foresighted enough to give a key to a neighbor when you decided on your home)—may be your real estate agent, if that person still has a key. If you're moving into an apartment house with a superintendent, of course, that person will have a key and can accept the shipment.

If possible, two people should watch the van being unloaded, checking the items against your copy of the inventory sheet and making a note of any damages. Don't sign the driver's copy of the inventory sheet until you have written on it every bit of damage and added (even if everything looks in perfect condition), "Subject to further inspection for concealed damage or loss." Don't let the driver or the agent convince you that signing the inventory is only a formality. Keep a record on your own inventory sheet of any damage or loss you have noted on the driver's sheet.

What can you expect the movers to do in unloading at no extra charge?

- They will lay the rugs where you want them.
- They will put the furniture in the rooms you want it in and in the location you indicate.
- They will put beds together.

They won't install your appliances or fixtures (such as chandeliers).

Don't let the movers get away with just dumping all your things inside the front door or inside the doors of the rooms. Don't let the movers convince you they have to leave earlier—and so can't lay rugs and so forth—in order to pick up another load. This may be true, but it isn't your problem—what you have paid for the move includes these services, and you're entitled to get them.

The same thing is true if you have arranged to have both packing and unpacking done by the movers. For some reason, a common experience of moving life is having the movers refuse point blank to unpack even though you arranged and will be paying for it. If persuasion doesn't work, write "No unpacking done" on the Bill of Lading and Certificate of Packing and Unpacking, which you will be asked to sign.

## WHAT IF THE VAN'S LATE?

What can you do to avoid being caught with enormous hotel or motel bills if the van is late? Unfortunately, delays of a week and over are almost a common matter on moves from one end of the country to the other.

Consider packing for camping out. If the family has had experience with actual camping, you're that far ahead, especially if you have equipment such as sleeping bags. This way, you can move into your new home and camp until the van arrives. There is also the possibility of saving money on motels (as we mentioned in Chapter 7, "Moving Yourself and Your Family") by camping on your trip to your new home if the weather is suitable.

Many people prefer to camp out while they wait for the van because, at least, they're in their new home. For families or individuals who have not had a chance to really study the layout of the new home, this means an opportunity to give real thought to exactly where furniture should be placed.

Other people would hate the idea of sleeping on the floor, no matter how comfortable the sleeping bag, and don't mind spending the money to stay in a comfortable hotel or motel. It is, of course, up to you.

## Claims Against the Movers

While we certainly hope that your move will be smooth and that everything will go beautifully, it may not, and you may have reason to make a claim against the movers. The Interstate Commerce Commission rules give you a period of nine months after the move in which to file a claim or add to one you have filed. On your claim you should list:

- the cost to replace (not the original cost) any missing or irreparably damaged item
- the cost of any repairs done, and estimates of repairs needed
- hotel and restaurant bills that you were forced to pay because the van was late

Send your claim either to the headquarters of the moving company or to the agent at your destination. If you have heard nothing after 30 days, complain to the local office of the Interstate Commerce Commission (see the telephone book under United States Government). If that doesn't work, write to:

Director of the Bureau of Operations
Interstate Commerce Commission
Washington, D.C. 20423

Scream again if the mover hasn't offered to settle with you in four months.

Be prepared for attempts to persuade you to accept a great deal less than you feel you deserve. Be prepared, too, for the movers to attempt to persuade you that any loss is your fault, A couple who lost a large quantity of liquor in a move, for instance, were told, "You should

*Send any breakage claims to either the moving company's headquarters or to the agent.*

never have given us that to move!"—but eventually were reimbursed for the entire cost of replacing the liquor. Don't be willing to settle for anything less than you deserve. You did, after all, pay liability insurance and you're entitled to the money.

## Be Sure . . .

Before you let the moving van drive away, be sure you have the following things:
>   driver's inventory (your copy)
>   name of the agent at your destination and address and telephone number, if possible
>   name of the driver of your van
>   number of the shipment
>   route the van will follow to your home

Be sure the driver has:
>   your exact and correct new address
>   an address and telephone number where you can be reached if you are not going at once to your new home

## Judging an Estimate

Judging an estimate means not only looking at the estimate when it comes from the movers but also knowing how it was made. These are the considerations to take into account.

**Care**—Estimator should examine all household goods, not just those on one floor or in one room, and should ask what is in cabinets and drawers rather than guessing.

**Price**—The estimate should have a logical price in relation to those given by other moving companies—beware of an extremely low estimate.

**Personality**—The personality of the estimator is perhaps the greatest intangible of all, but is helpful in judging a company. Choose a company with an estimator who seems honest and concerned about your move over a company with an indifferent estimator or one who was extremely insistent that he and his company know best.

## The Best Time to Move

The truth of the matter is that there is no best time to
move, but the chart below is designed to show the pros
and cons of moving at different times.

| Time | Pro | Con |
|---|---|---|
| *Summer* | Children can start new school in September; weather is relatively pleasant | This is busiest time for movers; delays are more likely during these months |
| *Winter* | Movers are less busy than at other times | Children must change schools in middle of year; weather may delay vans; goods may suffer damage due to weather in course of move |

# 6

# MOVING PLANTS AND PETS

Most of us are so accustomed to having plants and/or pets around us that it may not occur to us that there could be any problems in moving either or both. There are problems ranging from the question of how to move the plants and pets to whether your plants and pets will be allowed to enter your new state at all. (For a discussion of moving plants and pets outside the continental United States, see Chapter 12.)

In the first part of this chapter we will discuss moving plants and in the second part, moving pets.

## Should This Plant Move?

Before you decide to pack up all your favorite plants— both indoor and outdoor—find out the answer to the question, "Should this plant move?" The answer depends on the plant, your new home, and a couple of other circumstances.

Start by resisting the temptation (which people have been known to yield to) of digging up the nicest tree in your yard, loading it into your car, and driving off with it. In most cases, this is on the borderline between illegal and simply not very nice. If the home you're leaving is one you've sold, and one of the selling features was this particular tree, it's worse.

In any case, trees of this type, no matter how hardy they may seem, are not likely to last through a journey to a new location and replanting at their new home. There's more on moving trees below, but keep in mind that they are difficult to move even if they are in tubs rather than in the ground.

Shrubs, like trees, usually go with the property where you are living. In the case of both trees and shrubs there might be some possible justification for trying to move an expensive specimen you have planted on rented ground.

*When you move an outdoor plant be sure to dig a hole large enough to take the root ball with its soil without crowding.*

If you must move outdoor trees and plants keep the following rules in mind:

- All outdoor plants are extremely difficult to move. They tend to suffer all the symptoms of shock if they don't actually die.

- Do not try to move outdoor plants during the growing season. This is an almost guaranteed way of killing them.

- Move outdoor plants only in the fall, winter, and very early spring, when they are dormant. It's difficult to tell when outdoor plants are truly dormant, especially in fall and spring. Look for no leaves and no evidence that the plant is moving into a more active stage, such as small buds.

- When taking the plant out of the ground, be sure to cut a large enough area of soil so that the roots will not be injured in moving. Put the ball of soil inside a plastic bag with a little water for the move. Don't soak the roots, but don't let them dry out, either.

- When you and the plant reach your new home, dig a hole large enough to take the root ball with its soil without crowding. Before planting cut back the roots at their tips very slightly and cut back branches in the same way. This will keep the root and leaf systems from having to work too hard before the plant is established.

- Water thoroughly after planting and again anytime the ground is unusually dry.

Even if you follow these rules, don't be surprised if your transplanted plant makes a valiant start but comes to a pathetic end.

House plants pose fewer problems, but not as few as you might expect. While house plants aren't dug up and moved to a totally unfamiliar environment the way outdoor plants may be, they still are sensitive and may miss the home they were so accustomed to in your old city.

Many different elements make up the environment that causes some house plants to flourish and others to fade away—and the green thumb of the owner of the plants is just one of these elements. Light, humidity, nutrients, and heaven knows what other elements contribute to the healthiness of house plants. The plants in your home that have done well are the plants that have either adapted to your home or found the environment right from the start. The plants that were not suited to your home's environment died and were classed as failures.

If you keep in mind how sensitive plants are and the different elements that make up the environment, you can understand how much of a risk it is to move your plants. Add a journey with the change of environment and shaking up that it entails, and you can understand why very few house plants can be expected to move successfully.

This doesn't mean that you can't have the same terrific collection of house plants in your new home as you had in your old home, but it does mean you will have to try to reproduce the old environment as closely as possible, and it does mean you may have to try other plants if the old faithfuls don't prove so faithful. Before moving, compare your plants' environment in your old home with what it will be in your new home.

Is the sunlight the same? Not similar, but the same? How many hours of full sunlight do they get in your old home, how many hours of full sunlight will they get in your new home?

How humid is the air where your plants are growing

in your old home? Are they near a clothes washer or dishwasher, a dryer or a shower—anything that adds moisture to the air and helps the plants to grow better? Will your plants have similar amounts of moisture in the air in your new home?

Continue to analyze your plants' environment, step by step, and think again about which plants will definitely move—and which plants find other new homes.

## HOW DO PLANTS MOVE?

If you have an extremely valuable plant, don't try to move it yourself. Instead, call in professional plant specialists to discuss the practicality of such a move and to arrange to have the plant specialists move your plants.

Most plants, however, aren't that special, although if you have very strong feelings about a plant—one, for instance, that belonged to your great-grandmother and has been passed down through the family—it would be worthwhile to talk to the professionals. Get three opinions and three prices, even if you have to pay for the estimates, but choose the specialist on the basis of knowledge and experience rather than price.

The average house plant, however, doesn't need to be moved by plant professionals. Unfortunately, most professional movers won't take your house plants on the van—and if they do, they will not be liable for them. If you live fairly near your new home and have a car, you can make several trips back and forth for your plants; if you don't, and have a large collection, you will probably have to eliminate some from your life.

• If you are moving yourself by car, pack the plants in boxes without tops with lots of newspaper around them. Hold them on your lap.

● If you are moving yourself by plane or bus, you will be able to take fewer plants (too many are just too awkward) than you can take by car. Again, use newspaper around and between for protection, and carry the plants in shopping bags.

● If you are moving yourself by train, there is a possibility that your plants can go by train, too. This depends on the line, on the distance, and often on the individual at the railroad you first ask. If you want to take all your plants, it's definitely worth investigating.

● Give some thought to not taking more than one or two of your house plants. Instead, take cuttings, or whatever is the reproductive portion, of the others. Young, new plants from your old plants will have more vigor and be able to adjust to the conditions in your new home. And they certainly take less space to move.

Put the cuttings in plastic bags or wrap them in waxed paper and add a dampened piece of cotton. Try to plant them in soil as soon as you can—they'll stay alive for a while, but these conditions are a strain.

● Once the plants have arrived at your new home, give all the water-loving ones a good drink. They deserve it!

## MAY THIS PLANT MOVE?

Before you decide to move your plants and which plants to move, make sure that the state to which you are going will let your house plants in at all.

Some states that are having a problem with a specific type of plant pest will not permit plants that are attractive to that pest to enter the state, sometimes at all, sometimes without an inspection by state officials to be sure the house plant isn't infected already with the pest.

Other states either require a certificate of health from the home state (check with your County Extension agent for information on such a certificate) for private house plant owners, or require a certificate only for commercial house plant firms.

The states requiring certification of all house plants before they are let in are Florida, Montana, New Mexico, Oregon, South Carolina, Tennessee, Texas, Vermont, Washington, and Wyoming. Arkansas, which at present does not require such certification, may soon.

Louisiana requires a certificate if the plants are shipped on a moving van, and the other states either require certificates of plants shipped by or to commercial firms only, or do not require them at all. North Carolina, which does require a certificate from commercial firms, also requires it from private individuals if

*It may be easier to take cuttings than to move certain house plants. Place each cutting in a plastic bag with a dampened piece of cotton. Plant in soil as soon as possible.*

the plants are in pots 8″ or larger. (The 8″ is the diameter of the top of the pot.)

Both California and Arizona are fighting against the burrowing nematode and there are certain restrictions on house plants that are known to be popular with this pest. If you are bringing any of the following plants to California, bring them in a pot at least 4″ in diameter and 4″ deep; if you are bringing any of the plants into Arizona bring them in a pot at least 6″ in diameter. The soil will be sampled and, if the plant is found to be infested with the pest, the plant will be destroyed.

The plants that will be inspected include the following. Both the botanic name and the common name are given. In several cases, of course, these are the same.

Anthurium spp. Anthurium
Calathea spp. Calathea
Chamaedorea elegans (Collinia elegans)
                  parlor palm or Neanthebella palm
Dieffenbachia spp. ginger lily, garland flower,
                         or butterfly lily
Maranta spp. prayer plant
Monstera spp. Monstera or Ceriman
Musa spp. banana
Nephthytis Nephthytis (Syngonium)
Peperomia spp. Peperomia
Scindapsus spp. Pothos
Spathiphyllum spp. Spathiphyllum
Syngonium spp. tri-leaf wonder
Trichosporum spp. (Aeschynanthus) lipstick plant

Furthermore, if you're bringing any house plants to California from certain states or counties (Florida, Hawaii, and Cameron, Ellis, and Hidalgo counties of Texas) you must have a certificate that your plants are free of burrowing nematode.

Some plants can be grown both indoors and outdoors. If these come under various quarantines (citrus, for instance, and, among flowering plants, aster, chrysanthemum, zinnia, and dahlia) because of such pests as the European corn borer, they will be at least subject to inspection and at worst destroyed.

Whatever happens—even if after reading this you decide not to take any plants with you on your move—remember one thing: wherever you move there are sure to be plant stores.

## Should This Pet Move?

Plants find the move upsetting but rarely fade away because they miss their former owners. Pets, on the other hand, feel it's more important to be with you than to be in old familiar surroundings—or at least most pets feel that way.

The one exception to this rule is probably fish, and that is primarily because moving fish can be more complicated than it's worth. If your pets are fish, and expensive rare fish at that, a discussion with the store where you bought them is in order as soon as you know you're moving.

The best solution may be for the store to buy your rare fish back (don't be surprised if you are offered a good deal less than you paid in the first place). If this can't be worked out, the store may be able to suggest a firm that specializes in moving just such fish for commercial businesses but, again, this may prove a less than satisfactory solution because of cost. The best solution, sad though it seems, may be to give the fish to a fellow enthusiast.

Fish that aren't rare—pet goldfish, for instance—can

be transported by you in plastic bags. Test the bags for leaks well ahead of the time you put the fish in (some bags have slow leaks, which can leave the fish dry if not high). Several small bags will probably work better than one large bag (the weight of the water when you lift the bag could cause leaks to develop).

Don't try to move an aquarium with water and fish—either in your car or on the moving van. Again, there are too many chances of leaks developing.

Feed your fish at their regular mealtimes, change the water in the bags if the trip is a long one, and open the bags now and then to give the fish additional air. Don't be surprised if few—or none—of the fish survive the trip.

Some of the more exotic pets may require certificates to enter another state. Check with your veterinarian if you are planning to move a snake, a cheetah, or a monkey. Most states have few if any requirements for such common pets as rabbits, gerbils, hamsters, and white mice. Again, check with your veterinarian, who may know of some disease in the state to which you're moving which your pet should be inoculated against.

Move your monkey, cheetah, or other animal of this type under the most secure conditions possible—for the sake of your pet and everyone else. Moving these animals is a special matter, requiring a certain guaranteed temperature in the case of most, and probably a professional animal handler. Talk to the local expert on these animals—it may be your veterinarian, it may be someone at the local zoo, it may be a professional animal handler.

If birds are kept warm enough, they are usually good travelers and fairly easy ones. Move them in their cages with you. Some birds (your veterinarian will have a complete listing) are believed to be potential carriers of psittacosis, a disease that humans can catch from birds, and occasionally there will be a quarantine on these birds when the disease develops.

Cats usually prove themselves good travelers and, unlike most of the other pets listed in this section so far, they can move with you easily even if you are not driving to your new home. If you are driving, it is probably best to move your cat in a carrying case (you don't want it to suddenly leap out of the car and disappear, do you?). You can get carrying cases in pet stores, from branches of the ASPCA, or from your veterinarian.

*It is probably best to move your dog or cat in a carrying case. Fish can be transported in plastic bags; birds can be moved in their own cages.*

This is also true for dogs, although if your dog is very large you will probably have to have a case for him or her made to order. Be sure it will fit in the car!

You can assume that your pets will require some kind of health certificate and inoculations against rabies (back to the veterinarian). Again, check with the veterinarian who should be able to alert you to various special situations such as Hawaii's 120-day quarantine (you pay the kennel fee) to ensure your pet isn't "coming down with something," or Pennsylvania's requirement that you prove you own the pet.

Most pets can be shipped by air. In that case, the airline will tell you how to get them ready for shipment or will "pack" your pet for you. This method of traveling has the virtue for your pet of being fast, although it is not very comfortable. Arrange for someone to put your pet on the plane or pick up your pet at the airport if you will be driving and taking longer than the flight.

If your pets are traveling with you, don't forget their water and food dishes. And, of course, if their quarters are fairly cramped in your car, give them regular walks.

## STATE REGULATIONS CONCERNING HOUSE PLANTS

*Alabama*—no certification required

*Alaska*—no certification required but if shipped via Canada, plants will need a phytosanitary certificate (certificate that the plant is healthy)

*Arizona*—a long list of plants that are host to the burrowing nematode will be soil sampled (see text)

*Arkansas*—no certification required at present but law may be changed

*California*—as for Arizona (see text)

*Colorado*—certification only required of commercial growers

*Connecticut*—no certification required

*Delaware*—no certification required

*District of Columbia*—no certification required

*Florida*—requires a certificate of health for all house plants

*Georgia*—no certification required

*Hawaii*—no certification required but house plants may be inspected on arrival

*Idaho*—no certification required

*Illinois*—no certification required

*Indiana*—certification only required of commercial growers

*Iowa*—no certification required

*Kansas*—no certification required

*Kentucky*—no certification required

*Louisiana*—certification required only if shipped on a moving van

*Maine*—certification only required of commercial growers

*Maryland*—no certification required

*Massachusetts*—no certification required

*Michigan*—no certification required

*Minnesota*—no certification required

*Mississippi*—no certification required

*Missouri*—no certification required

*Montana*—requires a certificate of health for all house plants

*Nebraska*—no certification required

*Nevada*—no certification required

*New Hampshire*—no certification required

*New Jersey*—certification only required of commercial growers

*New Mexico*—requires a certificate of health for all house plants

*New York*—certification only required of commercial growers

*North Carolina*—house plants in pots 8" or larger should be certified; certification required of commercial growers

*North Dakota*—certification only required of commercial growers

*Ohio*—no certification required

*Oklahoma*—certification only required of commercial growers

*Oregon*—requires a certificate of health for all house plants

*Pennsylvania*—certification only required of commercial growers

*Rhode Island*—no certification required

*South Carolina*—requires a certificate of health for all house plants

*South Dakota*—no certification required

*Tennessee*—requires a certificate of health for all house plants

*Texas*—requires a certificate of health for all house plants

*Utah*—no certification required

*Vermont*—requires a certificate of health for all house plants

*Virginia*—no certification required

*Washington*—requires a certificate of health for all house plants

*West Virginia*—no certification required
*Wisconsin*—no certification required
*Wyoming*—requires a certificate of health for all
  house plants

In addition to the regulations listed above, plants
such as aster, calendula, chrysanthemum, mari-
gold, zinnia, and others that may be host to the
European corn borer need a certificate that they are
free of this pest if they are coming to Arizona or
California from a state with a corn borer infesta-
tion.

## It's a New Home for Your Plants, Too

The chart below is designed for you to fill out to decide
whether your house plants will be happy under new—
and different—circumstances. Keep in mind that an
increase in sunlight can be as great a shock to a plant as
a decrease, although the increase can be more easily
controlled.

|  | **Old Home** | **New Home** |
|---|---|---|
| Hours of sunlight |  |  |
| Humidity |  |  |
| Soil |  |  |
| Nutrients |  |  |
| (you can control) |  |  |

## Moving Your Pets

The following brief chart touches on some of the things to remember in moving your pet. Because pets are so different, however, this chart is by no means complete. You should consult your veterinarian as soon as you know of the move.

| Type of Pet | How to Move | Special Notes |
|---|---|---|
| Dog | With you in car; without you in plane, train | Evidence of rabies inoculation, other health certification often required |
| Cat | As for dog | Rarely needs health certification; consult veterinarian |
| Birds | In cage in car | May not be permitted into new state; consult veterinarian |
| Fish | Common: move in plastic bags with water | Rare: use specialist movers |
| Others | Consult veterinarian | Consult veterinarian |

# 10

# AFTER YOU GET THERE – WHAT ?

Well, it's finally happened—you and your possessions have met at your new home. In a sense, it's almost a matter of putting things back together again, but in the reverse order (everything that left your old home last should come into your new home first). The suggestions in this chapter apply whether you move with a professional van, with independent truckers, or on your own. In the section concerning unloading at the beginning of this chapter, there is material that applies only to professional movers.

This chapter has been divided into two sections. The first section lists the things that you should do first—such as making sure the electricity is turned on. The second section lists those things that can wait a little longer—such as hanging pictures. These priorities are not by any means absolute. They are just the order in which you may find things flow best.

## Up to the Door and Into Your Home

When the van or truck arrives with your household goods, be prepared to meet it with your copy of the driver's inventory and your own personal inventory (if

any). Check off the items on the inventory as they come
in the door of your new home. It helps to have at least
two people meeting the truck or van so that one can
check off items and the other can direct where items
should go.

If you are using professional movers, you are entitled
to have them lay the rugs and set up the beds. Be sure
they do so. Some people put up floor plans of their new
homes at the door so the movers can see where each
piece of furniture is to go (the furniture is shown on the
plan). If your opinions as to where the furniture should
go permanently are not yet jelled, at least be prepared
with a temporary place for each item.

If by any chance you have not already done so,

*It helps to have two people supervise the unloading of the
van or truck. One can check off the items while the other tells
the movers where the items should be placed.*

arrange to have someone expedite matters so you'll have electricity, gas (if any), and water.

If you have moved appliances, arrange now to have them connected if this requires a professional.

If the movers are unpacking for you, someone should watch to be sure they open cartons carefully. "Carefully" does not mean sticking a knife into the carton anywhere to slice it open—it's almost impossible not to hurt something when doing this.

Make the beds, or have someone else make the beds, as soon as possible.

Even though you've probably been eating in restaurants so much that it isn't a treat anymore, consider eating in one on moving-in day. Or go to the nearest grocery store and buy things for a make-your-own-sandwich supper.

## The Next Day

The next morning you can continue the process of arranging furniture and unpacking boxes.

If the move is made during the school year or just before it starts, arrange for the children's schooling if you haven't done so already.

If you have no mail in your new home, check with the post office to see if it is holding mail pending your arrival. If so, let the post office know you are ready for delivery.

If your appliances, including your stove, are connected, you can do major marketing today. And you may want to wash a load of clothes or take them to the laundry or launderette.

Introduce yourself to your new neighbors if you haven't met them already. Don't rush getting the house settled so much that you don't have time to learn about your new town and neighborhood.

If you are doing all your own unpacking, do it in stages based more or less on need.

The following is a suggestion of things to unpack first. This list isn't an absolute, it's just a list that has worked for other people. Some of these things you may not have packed.

- clock (unless someone has a traveling clock in the luggage that can be used until other clocks are unpacked)
- radio—so the family can hear the weather report for the day, find out what's going on in the world, and get a feeling for the new area in which you are living
- toiletries—shaving cream, razors, deodorant, toothpaste, toothbrushes
- coffeepot
- coffee
- saucepan
- frying pan
- clothing (so it won't be more wrinkled than necessary)

## Leave Until Later

As you live in your new home you'll find the way you view it changes with time. For this reason don't be completely inflexible when you arrange your household goods in it.

Many people recommend that you don't hang pictures until you've been living in your new home about six months. They've found from their own experience that it's hard to judge when you first move in where a picture "belongs." With time, you'll know exactly where you want it—and you won't have made unnecessary holes in the wall.

Mirrors are the same. Again, many people find it difficult when they first move into a new home to know where they will want mirrors. They wait until they are convinced they have found the perfect place before hanging them.

At the same time, it must be admitted that there is another school of thought about pictures and mirrors. These people feel that nothing "furnishes" a home as quickly as the accessories in it, and that to give everyone a feeling of home pictures and mirrors should go up as soon as possible.

*Give your new house the feeling of a home quickly by hanging pictures on the wall.*

It's up to you, of course, to decide what you want to do.

The entire question of unpacking is highly subjective. Some. people literally can't rest after a move until everything is unpacked and in its place. Others, although they may start off full of steam, slow down toward the end so that things remain in boxes for weeks or even years.

While the first method is undoubtedly efficient, it can leave everyone exhausted and cross for weeks. Some kind of blending of the two methods of unpacking— perhaps getting a room completely unpacked each weekend—seems to work best.

Don't rush into getting new curtains and draperies unless you need them desperately for privacy. Wait about a month until you know the various peculiarities of the different windows. A window with a beautiful view and no neighbors at all probably shouldn't have either a curtain or a drapery—unless the sun comes in with more force than you want all day and you'd like the option of shutting it out.

You may not be the type of person who likes to live with anything unfinished—in that case there's no reason why you shouldn't order your draperies the minute you choose your new home. But if you aren't that kind of person, give some thought to the possibility of waiting until you feel you know your home.

## Meeting People

There was a time when it was the custom for newcomers to a community to be called on and welcomed by the people who had lived there for years.

This custom died away, probably because so many of

us—twenty percent of all Americans—move every year. In some neighborhoods it would simply be impossible for the few old-timers to call on the large numbers of newcomers—they'd never be able to do anything else.

While the old way was nice, the new way makes more sense. This means that you can and should introduce yourself to your new neighbors. Furthermore, you should ask them questions. "What supermarket do you recommend?" is always a good opener.

Most people will be glad to answer questions like that and will probably give you other information at the same time, such as where to buy really good meat for a special meal, what department store (if any) has the best buys, and how many children are presently using your backyard as a short cut to school. (Let them go on using it, even if you'd hoped for a beautiful lawn, if you want to be at all popular.)

If you belong to a specific religion, join it in your new town, as we suggested earlier. If the town you have moved to is very small, this may be the only organizational affiliation you need, since in many towns most community life revolves around the various religions—and it doesn't matter socially which one, if any, you belong to.

In larger towns, there are other organizations you should look into that can help you get acquainted when you are first there and can offer worthwhile programs of service, education, or entertainment. Among them are:

• The Community Chest or United Fund. Calling on people for fund-raising drives is an excellent way to get to know your neighbors.

• The League of Women Voters (men may join, of course) where you can learn the political questions facing your new community in a non-partisan way and work for passage of legislation in which you believe.

• The parents' associations at your children's schools, so you can meet teachers and other parents easily.

• Your political party, if you are anxious to work for it (register to vote as soon as you can, though, whether or not you work for the party).

• The club for graduates of your college or university or, if there isn't one, an umbrella organization such as the American Association of University Women.

Many towns have quite intellectually oriented organizations that arrange for speakers. Keep your eyes and ears open and you'll learn about these. And, as we said in the chapter on children and the move, if there are newcomers' organizations, join them.

## SPORTS ACTIVITIES

More and more Americans are becoming more and more sports minded, and finding a place for sports may be one of your priorities once you're moved. Basically, there are three types of sports facilities. Some areas will have only one or two, and some may have none or only one offering one type of sport. Depending on the particular facility, the circumstances under which it was founded, its present board of directors, and (often the most important of all) size, these things can be either easy or not easy to join. For this reason, don't promise your kids or yourself certain sports until you've had a chance to investigate.

The types of facilities include:

• More or less traditional country clubs, featuring golf, tennis, dining facilities, dances. These clubs are often "exclusive" and proud of it, which means they are both extremely expensive and likely to have a long waiting list. You will probably need to be sponsored by at least two members and, although most of these clubs are becoming less capricious, you may be barred for reasons ranging from your religion to your lack of it.

These clubs usually have the best facilities (although some may be devoted to a single sport). Don't set your heart on joining one of these even if you belonged to a similar club in your other home (unless your club and this club have automatic membership-transfer privileges). In any case, you'll probably have a long wait for membership.

•Clubs devoted to a single sport (most often either swimming or tennis), usually with a smaller membership, often primarily from a neighborhood, and with much lower dues than the "big" clubs. These clubs usually have no dining facilities (although you can buy

*Joining a country club is one way to meet people in your new town or city.*

snacks) and membership is much easier. You may need sponsors, but the club will often find the sponsors for you. These clubs try to limit the size of their membership but waiting lists are usually shorter than at the traditional country club.

● Community sports facilities, which can range from wonderful to inadequate. These usually include a certain number of tennis courts (available either on a first come, first serve basis or by some kind of permit or sign-up list), swimming pools or lake or ocean swimming, and sometimes golf courses.

Don't snub the community facilities just because they're either free or very inexpensive. They usually have the same features as the private clubs and may even be better maintained.

If you are interested in sports, use whatever community facilities there are when you first arrive. As you get to know people, listen to what they have to suggest for any sports in which you are particularly interested.

Another point that should be taken into consideration is that different places are fascinated by different sports. Some areas are filled with tennis buffs, others with water skiing enthusiasts, others with cross-country snow skiers.

Living in an area that is very involved with a specific sport is the ideal chance for everyone in the family to learn a new sport—and to become if not expert, at least good at it. This can be a marvelous experience, and it is one of the compensations of moving.

## Exploring the Area

Don't spend all your time trying to get settled when you first arrive. This can be rewarding, but also exhausting. Instead, use some free time to get out and explore the area you have moved to, to find out what it is like, what surprises there may be, and what the most attractive places are.

You can do this with or without a car, in the country, in the city, or in the suburbs.

Start by walking around your own immediate neighborhood. Take different roads to see where they lead. You may find an unexpected brook, or a friendly neighbor two blocks away, or a marvelous, hidden restaurant.

You can explore by bus, too. Ride until you see something that looks interesting, get off, and find out more about it. Be sure, of course, to find out the route the bus will take coming back so you will know where to wait for it when you're ready to go home.

With a car, of course, you can go even farther afield. You can visit the state park that is near your new home, or just drive around the countryside.

You can also use the car to explore the shopping facilities in your area. Many people live months in a place without knowing that by driving five miles in another direction they could save money on food, or find a wonderful farmers' market or a place that makes maple syrup or fabric and sells it wholesale.

If there's a local historical society with guided trips to various areas of interest, consider joining it. This is an excellent way to put some flesh on the bones of the area you're seeing.

And, of course, the more you get to know your new surroundings, the more at home you're likely to feel.

## The Local Papers

Wherever you move, be sure you read the local newspapers and tune in to the local radio and TV stations.

If you want to continue to get the paper from your former home that's fine—it can keep you up to date with what is going on there—but you are now living in another area and should be informed about that area.

Many newspapers, especially those with a relatively small circulation, can give you a much better impression of life in the area than months of trying to figure it out for yourself can do. Often, these newspapers tell what everyone knows already—that the high school had a picnic, and the women at the church cooked a chicken supper, and that the Smith family had relatives staying with them for a week. Putting these things in the paper somehow makes them seem more important— and why not?

Use the paper, then, and the radio and television to get some idea of the pace of life in your new community and to keep up to date with what is going on. If you get the paper, there's no chance of your missing the strawberry festival on the green when that comes around; without it, you might not know because no one would think to mention it to you.

## Be Yourself, Of Course

If you move into a community where the people are extremely different from you, or seem that way, there's no point in making yourself over to be like them. For one thing, you wouldn't succeed, and for another you wouldn't be happy.

The United States is so homogeneous today that you probably won't find much difference between your old area and your new one, but there are a few enclaves where customs are slightly different and, if these manners don't come to you easily, you can be miserable if you try to change yourself.

At the same time, it's a mistake to be uncompromising. We all know people who have lived in a place for thirty years or so—but still wish they didn't.

• Speech. You might as well accomodate your speech to the speech of the area. Don't change the way you talk, but slow it down a little if it's too fast for the natives to understand, and speed it up a little if it's too slow. Watch for local pronunciations ("crik" for "creek") and use them. Why not? It will save time and repeating yourself.

• Friendliness. The casual kind of friendliness that you have (or don't have) in the supermarket varies surprisingly in different parts of the country. If you move to an area where everyone is so friendly you can't believe they're sincere, suspend your disbelief and go along with it.

If you move to another area where everyone is so cold you get frostbite every time you go into the market, you really have to decide for yourself what to do. We'd be inclined to be friendly—maybe they'll learn from you.

• Hospitality. The hospitality of one area can seem overwhelming to someone from another area, and one area can seem very cold to someone from a more hospitable place.

Until you find out what the custom is where you've moved, face the fact that in many places people "drop in" (rather than telephoning first) and tend to stay. Be prepared with cake or cookies to offer with coffee or tea.

By the same token, if you're from a drop-in area don't assume you've moved to one. And don't wonder why people don't drop in on you—it may be an area where people only drop in on each other in time of trouble.

In any case, while it may all seem very unfamiliar at

first, you'll find in about three to six months that, although you may still be aware of the differences between your old home and your new home, you will no longer be startled by them.

## Commercial Welcoming Organizations

We've left commercial welcoming organizations for last because relatively few communities have them. These organizations send someone around to see you when you first move in, usually within the first week. The person sent combines two roles—that of a person living in the community who can advise you on various matters such as schools (if you aren't already settled on

*Be prepared with cake or cookies in case a new neighbor drops in to welcome you.*

a school) and that of a person who, by means of free samples and discount tickets, will introduce area merchants to you.

Since these people are paid by the merchants they represent, their view of the local shopping scene tends to be somewhat slanted. If, however, you keep that in mind, the noncommercial information the welcomer can give you can be very helpful, especially if it's a person with whom you have some feeling of rapport.

There's nothing wrong with these commercial welcoming organizations, provided you realize that they do have a business purpose.

In some communities (again, relatively few) the clubs for newcomers have members who make personal calls on new arrivals in the community. These visits are extremely useful—and you'll often get the best information from these people—as well as not having any commercial taint.

Whatever the case, don't turn down any offers of information in your new community. You can, after all, always evaluate it on your own—and what have you got to lose?

# 11

# LETTING PEOPLE KNOW

One of the biggest chores of moving, and one that most of us don't think too much about when a move is first mentioned, is letting people know that you now have a new address. We've already touched on this subject in earlier chapters, but in this chapter we go into the matter in more detail. You'll also find lists of some of the individuals and organizations who should be notified.

## Types of Notification

Start by deciding what kind of notification you want to use. Postcards are practical, as all the information is in a fairly narrow space, people can post them on a bulletin board, and with only a little trimming of the edges they'll fit in most file boxes. There's another important point, too—postcards cost less to send than letters.

Some people, however, for one reason or another, prefer to send a letter notifying friends of the change of address. This can be in the form of a Christmas letter, for instance, if the timing is right, and can include the family news of the previous year along with the new address and new telephone number. You can use post-

**185**

cards for "official" notifications to firms and individuals who really don't need to know anything but the basic information.

There is one problem with including the news of a move in a Christmas letter—or adding it to a Christmas card—and that is that people are often asleep at the switch around the holidays. These people will open your letter or card, may even make some remark about the fact that you've moved or are moving when they send you your Christmas card, but completely forget to make any note in an address book or file that you have a new address.

For this reason, to be safe, you should probably stick with postcards, either the ones furnished by the post office or ones you have made especially for you. You can use your Christmas letter or card to remind people, if you want.

The cards furnished by the post office are, as we mentioned earlier, not terribly attractive, but they do have the virtue of being free. If you plan to design your own card, they can help remind you of the information to include, and in any case you should use the official card for notifying the post office itself just to keep the post office happy.

The post office cards come in packets containing eight postcards on which to notify individuals or firms and one card on which to notify the post office itself. Eight cards are not very many, but the post office has apparently been told not to be generous with these packets. You may find yourself forced to go back again and again to some offices, or to send different members of the family to get more cards.

During the last month in your old home, as magazines arrive, tear off the address label and paste that to the postcard in the "old address" place. If you know more than a month in advance that you are moving, of course, start doing the pasting of these labels two months ahead. Most magazines and other publications ask for six weeks notice of a change of address but seem to be able to cope with four weeks.

The special postcard for the post office is printed in black in the post office package rather than blue as are the other cards. The post office card requires the same information everyone else does—old and new addresses—but has other sections, too. These ask you whether or not you're willing to pay postage for the forwarding of third class mail, newspapers, and magazines—one year for third class, 90 days for the magazines and newspapers. Check the "yes" box—the postage isn't that much and you might miss something interesting.

Some firms have a little note to the post office at the top of their envelopes reading "Address correction requested." These firms are so anxious not to lose track of you that if you move without letting them know about it they'll pay the post office for notifying them. This explains why you are likely to continue to get a lot of mail order catalogues even though you didn't write to the firms to give your new address.

If only one member of the family is moving it may be best, except perhaps in a town where everyone in the post office really does know everyone in the town, not to give the post office a change of address. It seems to be difficult for the post office to resist the temptation to forward all the mail with the particular last name they're alerted for. It's better to impose on the people left at the old homestead to make liberal use of your own change-of-address cards to businesses and individuals, and to tell people when you get the opportunity.

As we mentioned earlier, you can buy change of address cards in a stationery store, or have ones made to your taste by a printer (if you're looking for a printer, the printer of the local newspaper is the logical place to start) if you don't like the ones the post office offers.

The problem with both change of address cards you buy and ones you have printed is that you run the risk of leaving out something—such as your name. Any change of address notification should include the following information:

- your first name, middle name or initial (if used), last name
- your old address—number and street, apartment number (if any), PO Box or RD number
- your city, state, and zip code (old)
- your new address—number and street, apartment number (if any), PO Box or RD number
- your city, state, and zip code (new)
- the date the new address takes effect ("at once" is fine)
- your account number (to be written in by hand for those institutions where you have an account number)
- your new area code and telephone number (if you know them)

The advantage to having printed cards made over using the post office cards or ones you buy in a stationery store is that the information listed above can all be printed on the cards. That way, you only have to address the cards, not fill out all the change of address information, too.

If you have any relatives or friends who are likely to consider a printed card cold you can add a little note if you want—but most people realize how much time moving itself takes and will just be pleased to be sent the card itself.

Under certain circumstances, you will want to tell some people in person that you are moving. This is true, of course, with most of your close friends living nearby, with the neighbors you are leaving behind (who will also want to know a little about the people taking your place, if you have met them), and with certain trades-people in stores you shop in regularly—the drugstore, the supermarket, and so on.

There's no need to send such people a change of address notice unless you think you want to keep in touch with them after you move. In the case of a small store where you have a charge account and might have purchases that aren't billed when you leave, the change of address notice is a good idea.

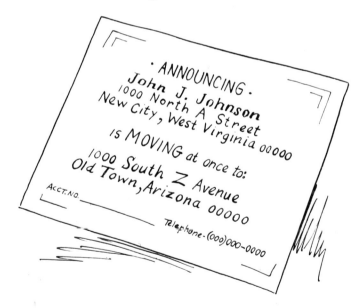

*Change of address cards are a good way to notify family and friends that you are moving.*

Whether or not you are sending these people actual notification, however, it is polite to tell them yourself that you are moving when you know you are. The important thing here is to allow enough time for the telling, for their questions, exclamations, expressions of sorrow that you're leaving, and for your own expressions of gratitude for past favors. These good-byes can provide some of the nicest memories of your old community and be among the pleasantest parts of your move.

## When to Notify People

If you know six months ahead of time that you'll be moving and your exact address, it may be tempting to send out notification as soon as you can. Don't. It's far too easy for people either to put the notification aside until the date when it is to go into effect and forget all about it, or to ignore the date and send everything to the new address too far ahead of time.

Start notifying individuals and organizations about six weeks in advance of the move (there's no reason in the world if you know your new address earlier why you can't start addressing cards). Start with magazines, book clubs, and other publications and go on from there.

The following listing is arranged with the first to be notified at the top. Some will be notified in writing, some by telephone, and some in person, depending upon the particular situation.

●Magazines, book clubs, other publications (include address label on change of address notice if possible).

●Movers, if you are using professional movers to move you from one state to another. If you are moving within your own state you probably won't need to give much more than a week's notice, but find this out once you know where you will be moving.

● Insurance companies, including hospital, health, accident (can these policies be transferred to your new company if your move involves a change of employer?), fire, home (can these policies be transferred to your new home as soon as you take possession?), automobile (will the rates change in your new state?), life, any other.

● Veterans Administration.

● Social Security Administration.

● Utility companies, so they can either turn off the utilities in your old home or transfer the account to another name. Also be sure the utility companies in

*The best way to notify local store owners that you are moving is in person.*

your new home city are notified. Utilities include electricity and sometimes gas and water. Remind the companies of the action you want taken a week before the
move to make sure the action is taken. Get the name of
the person taking the information from you for follow-
up purposes.

- Telephone company, as for utilities, above.
- If you have deposits with either a utility company
or the telephone company, be sure they have your new
address so they can refund it to you. You can try to get
the refund before you leave your old home, but it isn't
likely you'll succeed.
- If you are very pleased with your doctor, or if you
have some condition that requires frequent visits, notify your doctor of your move and ask for suggestions
for doctors in your new city. If not, you can let this go
until you find a new doctor in your new town who can
write your former doctor for your charts.
- The same thing applies to your dentist. Again, if you
are pleased or making regular visits, let your dentist
know you are moving and ask if he or she can suggest a
colleague in your new town. Otherwise, wait until you
have found a dentist and have him send for your charts.
- Any other professionals—lawyers or accountants,
for instance, with whom you have worked closely—
should be told about your move.
- If you have an account at a brokerage office, arrange
to have it transferred to a firm in or near your new city.
- If you want, you can arrange to have your local
credit bureau send your rating to the credit bureau in
your new city. Do not do this unless you know
definitely—preferably by having seen the records—that
your credit rating is a good one. Credit bureaus must let
you know your rating now if you ask. If you have a poor
rating, there's no reason to have it sent to your new

town. You may be able to build up a better one in your new location.

• Organizations, especially ones with branches in your new area and particularly if the organizations have special qualifications for membership.

• Your religious group. If your religion permits members to move from one congregation to another by means of a letter of transfer, be sure to ask for one when notifying your religious leader of your move.

• Relatives (or at least the ones you write to). Notify close relatives in person, by telephone, or by a personal letter, less close relatives by card or whatever means you have chosen to notify most of your friends.

• Friends. Use your Christmas card list (if you have one) as well as your address books for this.

*Once you know you are moving you may want to notify friends and relatives by telephone.*

• Your children's school (if the move is made when the schools are open). Visit the school in person to arrange to have the records sent to the new school or taken with you. If the move is made when school is not in session, or if you are in a terrible rush, or if you don't know where the children will be going to school, this can all be done by long distance telephone or by mail.

• Since only one thing is surer than taxes you can be reasonably certain that the tax authorities will find you when you move, whether or not you tell them you're going. However, to make life easier all around, notify the state, federal, and city (if your city has taxes) tax authorities and the motor vehicle bureau that you are moving and where.

• Notify those companies that deliver to you on a regular basis (milk, water softener, diaper service, bakery) and give them your new address so they can send you a final bill if necessary.

• If you want, you can notify stores where you have charge accounts that you are moving. If you are short of time, however, this really isn't necessary—you can notify them when you get your next bill (it will be forwarded from your old address).

• If you have borrowed money from any concern—a bank or finance company—let them know of your move.

## FORWARDING MAIL

The post office at your old address will forward first class mail, at no charge to you, for a year. After the year is up, the forwarding stops.

This is why it is a good idea to reinforce the fact of your move in the minds of your friends and relatives (they seem to be the biggest offenders) who may have received your change of address notice but not made any note of your new address.

This is the time when a Christmas card or Christmas letter can be valuable—when the time comes to tell people a second time that you have moved.

In the Christmas letter, do a paragraph on how you like your new home and include the new address in the body of the letter as well as on the envelope. Maybe they'll remember to write it down this time.

On a Christmas card, just put your address under your signature and, for people who may not be as observant as you would like, write "Note."

## KEEP A RECORD

In any case, do keep some kind of record of the people you notify of the move—by telephone, in person, or with a change of address card—to avoid overlooking anyone or duplication.

The record needn't be, and probably shouldn't be, complicated. The easiest thing to do is just to use a check mark next to the firm or individual's name in an address book. For a firm you don't list in an address book, such as the telephone company, an abbreviation such as "phone" would make it clear that the telephone company has been notified at least once. (Incidentally, in the case of the telephone and utilities companies it may be a good idea not only to telephone your instructions but also to put them in writing, with a carbon copy you can keep.)

If you follow the system of keeping track of just which firms and individuals have been notified of your move, every member of the family who is old enough to write can help with addressing the cards. It's too big a job for one person to do alone if there are others around who can help.

## Firms and Individuals to Notify

The following chart lists some of those firms and individuals who should be notified of your move, arranged more or less in the order in which they should be notified. Some should be told by telephone, some in person, and some with a change of address card. See the text.

| Firm or Person (list) | When to Notify | Check When Done |
|---|---|---|
| Magazines | 6 weeks ahead | |
| Book clubs | 6 weeks ahead | |
| Other publications | 6 weeks ahead | |
| Movers | 6-8 weeks ahead | |
| Insurance companies | 4 weeks ahead | |
| Veterans Administration | 6 weeks ahead | |

| Firm or Person (list) | When to Notify | Check When Done |
|---|---|---|
| Broker | 3 weeks ahead | |
| Credit bureau | 3 weeks ahead— only if desired | |
| Organizations | 2 weeks ahead | |
| Social Security Administration | 6 weeks ahead | |
| Gas company | 4 weeks and 1 week ahead | |
| Electric company | 4 weeks and 1 week ahead | |
| Telephone company | 4 weeks and 1 week ahead | |
| Water company | 4 weeks and 1 week ahead | |
| Doctor | 3 weeks ahead or before | |
| Dentist | 3 weeks ahead or before | |
| Lawyer, accountant | 3 weeks ahead or before | |

| Firm or Person (list) | When to Notify | Check When Done |
|---|---|---|
| Religious group | 2 weeks ahead | |
| Relatives | 2 weeks ahead | |
| Friends | 2 weeks ahead | |
| Schools | 2 weeks ahead | |
| Tax authorities | 2 weeks ahead | |
| Milk | 1 week ahead | |
| Water softener | 1 week ahead | |
| Diaper service | 1 week ahead | |
| Bakery | 1 week ahead | |
| Charge accounts | 1 week ahead | |
| Bank, finance company | 1 week ahead | |

# 12

# MOVING OUT OF THE CONTINENTAL UNITED STATES

Not only are more and more of us moving every year, more of us are moving farther, including outside the continental United States—either to another part of the United States or to a foreign country.

From one point of view, there is very little difference between moving from one end of the state to the other and moving outside the continental United States. For both types of move, you have to decide what to take and what to leave, you have to decide who will pack and how things will be packed, and you have to decide how to move. From other points of view the difference between moves is tremendous.

## Moving to Alaska or Hawaii

If you are moving to Alaska or Hawaii your main problems will involve the distances that must be traveled and the relative difficulty in reaching these places.

Alaska can be reached fairly easily by road from certain parts of the United States, notably those near the Canadian border, which means a moving van may prove the obvious way to move your household goods. Furthermore, the moving company will know all about

**199**

taking your household goods through Canada "in bond" so they do not have to clear either Canadian or American customs.

If you are moving to Alaska from somewhere near either ocean, check into the possibility of sending your things by ship. Shipment by sea is almost always less expensive than shipment by road.

If you're moving to Hawaii, your large pieces of furniture will go by sea no matter what; you may want to fly some items that are smaller.

Don't assume that the rules and rates for flying property are the same for these states (or other offshore places) as they are for inside the continental United States. Check with the airline well before making final plans.

Traveling light is even more important when you are moving to Alaska or Hawaii than it is when you are moving to the other side of the continental United States. Shipping anything to places this distant is expensive by any method and you may find that it makes more sense to buy new furniture. Even though it may be priced higher than in the continental United States, it may be more convenient and more suitable to the area than to take all your furniture from home.

If your stay will be a relatively short one (two years, say) and you're extremely fond of your furniture but don't want to take it all with you, you might consider putting it in storage, although as we mentioned earlier, storage is one place where furniture is more likely to be damaged or to disappear.

Sea shipment used to be a somewhat complicated matter, but with the arrival of containers, trucks that take containers, and container ships, it has been greatly simplified. A truck with a container (it's a huge rectangular box) will pull up outside your house and movers will pack the container so it is prepared for life on the bounding main.

This type of moving is handled by most of the professional movers and also by firms that specialize in packing and shipping household goods overseas. Look for these in the yellow pages of the telephone book of larger towns under "Packing."

Aside from the physical move itself, moving to Alaska or Hawaii is no different from moving anywhere else in the United States. Your automobile, for instance, can be driven to Alaska or shipped to Hawaii (but check the price of buying a car there, and consider leaving or selling your present car). There are no problems with electrical current or currency, and you can bring your pet (although your pet will be in a kennel for 120 days—at your expense—in Hawaii).

*Moving to Alaska need not be more complicated than moving to any other location in the continental United States.*

## Moving to a Foreign Country

Moving to a foreign country is quite different from moving within the United States, whether the continental United States or not.

Start by getting as much information about the country as you can from the consulate of that country— usually located in the nearest large city. If there is no consulate, write to the country's embassy ("Embassy of Ruritania, Washington, D.C."). Explain that you plan to emigrate there (if you plan to live there forever and become a citizen) or become a permanent resident (if you don't plan to become a citizen).

This should result in a flood of brochures, leaflets, and letters to you. Don't be surprised if a country that was thrilled to have you as a tourist isn't enchanted at having you permanently—the material the United States sends to would-be immigrants has a similar tone.

Check carefully the laws governing the employment of foreign nationals (that's what you will be if you move, at least until you become a citizen, which takes years). Unless you are being moved by your employer who is already established in the country, you may find you are forbidden to work at all.

Once you've worked out that primary problem (perhaps you've retired), look for information concerning electrical current. This will determine what, if any, electrical appliances you can and should take with you. Many parts of the world, for instance, have current at 220 volts, in contrast to the current in the United States which is 110 volts. This means your American appliances will be burned out if plugged into this current.

The United States current is 60 cycles; other parts of the world (even some which have 110 volts) often have

50-cycle current. This affects the running of certain electrical appliances, including clocks.

Most of the United States now has a.c. current (alternating current) rather than d.c. (direct current). Other parts of the world, on the other hand, may have d.c.

Most of these differences in current have been studied by enterprising people who have come up with various kinds of adaptors to solve these problems. These are not altogether satisfactory and you should give very serious thought to the possibility of selling or giving away the appliances you presently own in the United States—and all other items that run on electrical current, unless they are specifically designed for use anywhere in the world.

*Traveling light is important when you move long distances.*

In most parts of Mexico, for instance, where the voltage is the same as in the United States, the current is 60 cycles a.c. However, in Mexico City, Pachuca, Tlalnepantla, and the areas surrounding these places, the current is 50 cycles a.c. This is a relatively minor problem, and may not affect any of your appliances. If it does affect one or two, you may be able to correct the problem with an adaptor, but it is something you should be aware of before moving appliances.

The next thing to check in the information you will receive from the consulate or embassy of the country to which you hope to move is how customs affects citizens or immigrants. Because you are moving into the country, forget how friendly customs was when you were a tourist. In the position you're in now you're considered the same as a native of the country—and customs everywhere is always harder on the natives.

In many cases you'll find that, in order to encourage local industry, customs duties will be 100% or more of the value of something. If this is the case with the country to which you are moving, it would obviously be to your advantage not to bring these items with you— unless they are things that are absolutely unobtainable in your new country and you are convinced you can't live without.

### PAPERWORK

Once you have read all the booklets, brochures, and regulations pertaining to your intended move, your work isn't over. Yards and yards of paper—forms of one kind and another—will follow.

Make sure first of all that the country where you want to live is willing to let you live there. Don't just go to the country until you either have whatever documents are necessary or have ascertained that no documents are needed.

Once you have the documents needed for moving yourself to the new country, find out what else you will need.

You will need U.S. Export Form 7525-V, which is a Shipper's Export Declaration. This is usually made out in quadruplicate before you leave the United States. If you are using a professional mover for your shipment, find out if the driver of the van can execute this document for you before your household goods cross the border or go off to sea.

If you are taking with you some valuable (worth more than, say, $200) foreign-made items, such as a watch or camera, and you plan to come back to the United States someday (well, you do, don't you?), it's a good idea to

*When you move to a foreign country you have to declare all the household goods that you are bringing in with you.*

register them with U.S. Customs before you leave the country. This is especially true if there's a possibility that you may return to the United States permanently. The reason is that foreign-made items can be, in theory, considered dutiable over and over again unless you can prove that you owned the item before you ever left.

Register these items by taking them to the customs office nearest you. If there isn't one near you, you can wait until you are actually leaving the country or take some proof of your ownership date of purchase with you to use when you come back.

When you get to your destination you will have to declare all the household goods that you are bringing in with you. If you made an inventory of your own use that; if you did not, you will have to use the one made by the professional movers. This may actually have an advantage, of course; if the movers marked your goods as being older than they are your customs duties may be lower than they would be if the customs officials went by the actual age.

It almost pays to be dirty when it comes to bringing household goods into some countries. Appliances, for instance, that are extremely well kept or that are packed in their original cartons are more than likely to be valued by Mexican customs as "new." If you feel you must clean appliances before you leave the United States for Mexico, in other words, don't do too good a job of it—leave some traces that the things have been used.

Some countries require the owner of the goods to go through customs with them. Other countries want you to be in the country with a permanent home before their customs agents will look at your shipment. This is something to find out about in detail—even if you really have to keep after the consul. Don't feel badly about this—he or she is paid by the people of the country to help establish good relations with the United States and its citizens.

## THE EXTRAS

Unless someone else (an organization, for instance) is picking up the bill, moving to another country is likely to be extremely expensive. For one thing, you don't have the same options for the moving itself that you have if you are staying home, although you can, of course, always decide to sell or give away all your household goods and start over in the new country, buying things there. If you are tempted to do this, it's worth figuring out what the real essentials of your life are, and then finding out what they would cost to replace in your new home as compared to what they would cost to bring with you and pay duty on.

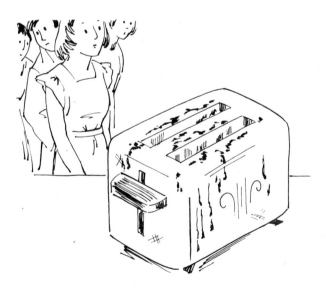

*Appliances should look as if they have been used so that they won't be valued as "new" by customs inspectors.*

If traveling very light indeed doesn't appeal to you, you will almost certainly have to use professional movers because of their expertise. While you will be prepared for the expense of the professional movers, there will probably be a lot of extras for which you may not be so prepared.

●Forget everything you ever experienced at customs and be prepared to spend a great deal of time getting your household goods through customs and a great deal of money on the final levy.

Different countries have different attitudes toward personal checks and traveler's checks—and whether or not they'll accept either in American dollars.

Find out ahead of time (back to the consul) what the country you are moving to will want.

●Some countries have arrangements with customs brokers of their own nationality at the border—these people act as brokers for all household goods shipments. (Mexico has this type of arrangement.) There is a charge (around $2 to $3 per 100 pounds for most countries) for the services this broker provides in helping the shipment clear the border.

●There may be a charge by the agent of the mover you are using for the same purpose. This charge is about the same—$2 to $3 per 100 pounds.

●"Hidden" charges that suddenly pop up at you include such things as "import charges" (charged by the country you are entering) and "export charges" (charged by the country you are leaving). You don't get anything (except the right to continue on your way) from these charges, which again run around $2 to $3 per 100 pounds, but the countries involved have a nice source of revenue and, presumably, someone's taxes are lower.

• Storage charges. Despite everything this book has said about putting your household goods into storage— mainly "Don't do it"—you may find it necessary to store them in the course of a move outside the United States. This is because in many countries there are simply not enough moving vans to go around, to take your household goods from an American van or from a ship and carry them to your destination.

• Food and shelter. Because of the time it often takes for household goods to get from one part of the world to another, you should be prepared to spend weeks in a hotel of some kind or camping out in your home in your new country.

In addition to the "normal" delays in delivering things in the United States, shipments outside the United States are subject to additional delays caused by distance, weather, and dock strikes, which can last for months and have their effects felt for months afterward.

Either be prepared with vast quantities of money for the living quarters and meals you will need while you wait, or plan to make the best of things by camping out in your new home.

## YOUR PLANTS AND PETS

If your heart is tied to a plant in your home, forget about moving outside the United States. Plants will have to be left behind. All countries are extremely strict about permitting plants to enter. If you try to bring in a plant, or a cutting, or a root, or a bulb, it will be destroyed by customs officials.

There is one way to get around this with most countries—get in touch with the equivalent of the Department of Agriculture and obtain a permit to import a plant. This is extremely difficult to arrange in most countries and is very rarely granted to individuals—but you can always try.

Your pets are likely to have an easier time of it, although in some countries your dogs may be quarantined for as long as six months at your expense. There are restrictions on the admission of birds into some other countries. Most nations want your pet to be accompanied by a certificate of health from your veterinarian. Dogs are often required to have a certificate that they have been given rabies inoculations within the last year.

## COMING BACK

Contrary to what you might expect, the customs officials of the United States do not weep tears of joy when Americans who have been living outside the United States come back again. There may be a "Welcome home" greeting, but there are lots of rules and regulations, too. By and large, though, it's easier (and in terms of duty often less expensive) to come home than it was to leave.

You can bring back, without duty, the household goods you took with you, those you bought in the other country if they have been used for a year, all your American-made clothes, and the foreign items you registered with U.S. customs when you left. Any other items will probably have duty levied on them, although you do have a certain personal exemption which varies from time to time.

You will need U.S. Customs Form number 3299, which is a declaration for free entry of household goods. The United States does not require that you and your goods enter at the same time, and you'll probably precede them. When you enter, tell the customs official that you have unaccompanied goods following. The official will then give you form 3299—if he or she doesn't, ask for it or get it at any customs office.

## Moving Outside the United States

Don't just jump up and go to your favorite country to live (you'll probably be turned back at the border); instead, plan a move as big as that carefully in advance. Following is a listing of points to cover—it is by no means exhaustive but it will give you a start.

Is working permitted for non-citizens in your new home?

If it is, do you have the work permit needed?

If it isn't, do you have other income?

Have you chosen your home?

Have you received permission to live in country?

Have you obtained United States export form?

Have you packed your household goods?

Have you shipped your household goods?

Have your goods passed customs?

Have your goods been delivered to your new home?

# 13

# THE FINANCIAL SIDE

In addition to the various expenses that have been touched on already in this book, it is quite likely that moving will have an effect on your tax picture. This won't necessarily be a negative one, since the income tax laws make allowance for moving expenses—provided they are in connection with your job or business (your employer transfers you or you accept a new job) and provided the change of the location of the job would require you to travel at least 35 miles farther to work if you had not moved.

For this reason, keep a list of your expenses in connection with your move (use the chart at the end of this chapter). Even if your employer is "paying" for the move you will probably find that the amount you are reimbursed is less than the move actually costs you.

The amount your employer gives you for moving expenses must, of course, be reported on your income tax as income, but your moving expenses can be deducted from the total.

## What You Can Deduct

• You can deduct your round-trip expenses for going to your new city to look for a new home. You can't

212

deduct expenses until you have a job but once you do, even if it is a new job, your expenses of looking for a home are deductible. This includes food, lodging, and transportation. The main reason for the trip must be to look for a new place to live.

• You can deduct the cost of moving your household goods and personal items from your old home to your new one.

• If you owned your home and sold it, you can deduct the costs of selling your old home and buying a new one. If you did not own your old home, you can deduct expenses connected with settling your lease and arranging for a new one for your new home.

Deductible expenses include commissions (such as to real estate agents), cost of advertising, such things as state transfer taxes, the cost of appraisals, legal fees of various kinds in connection with the change from one home to another. You may not deduct the cost of repairs or the amount (if any) you lose on selling your former home.

• You may deduct the cost of your food and lodging at your new city for up to 30 days after you have found a job, and while waiting to move into your new home.

Some of these deductions are limited to a certain amount, so don't let anyone encourage you to fling your money around on the theory that "You'll get it all back anyway."

Keep receipts (be sure the date is included) for all the expenses listed above. The Internal Revenue Service may never challenge your moving expenses, but if it does it will be much easier for everyone if you can produce evidence of all (or almost all) of the expenses.

If you have an Internal Revenue Service office near you, it may be worthwhile stopping in (not at the busiest time of the year, but a little before) to get a booklet called "Tax Information on Moving Expenses" (the title may change from year to year).

• If you want to qualify for the deductions, don't be in a hurry to move away from your new home and place of business. You must work full time near your new location for at least 39 weeks during the 12 months that follow the move.

This doesn't mean you must stay with a terrible employer, though—you don't have to stay with the employer who "caused" the move, only in the area you have moved to. You can change employers if you want, provided you stay in the area.

Tax Information on Moving Expenses, *a booklet available from the Internal Revenue Service, tells you what moving expenses are tax deductible.*

# What Will the Move Cost?

What can you figure as being the actual cost of the move?

Unfortunately, there is no way of telling you exactly what your move will cost. Too many different factors enter into determining the final bill for a move.

If you move light, and move only a short distance, you can make it (by doing all the work yourself or with friends) for well under $200, including having the rug cleaned.

If, on the other hand, you are moving across the country, own a lot, and you want everything including the packing done for you, you should figure on something more like $10,000—and even that might not be enough.

In your particular case, a lot will depend on how willing you are (or how able) to trade your own time and muscle for money.

Most people who are being moved by their employer in a situation where the employer is paying for "everything" including packing, take full advantage of this situation. One company, moving its people from one suburban area surrounding a large city to another surrounding the same city, found the average move came in at just under $2,000. Big houses with lots in them were more expensive to move people from and into—there the figure hit around $6,000.

Company-paid moves are, we suspect, bound to be more expensive than moves for which the individual family pays the bill. If the company's paying, most people will be delighted to have the movers pack, even the simplest things. Then, too, it's unlikely anyone will be watching the movers in such a case to be certain everything is done in the most economical way.

● Don't assume that your company won't pay for your move just because, as far as you know, they haven't done so in the past. Try to make payment for a move part of the compensation package of your new position.

● Don't be too quick to accept a flat amount for moving from your company. Try to keep the amount the company will pay open ended if at all possible.

● If you are taking a job with a new company in a new area, try to bargain things so that the full cost of the move is part of the deal.

● Don't think you must spend the amounts listed in order to move. Go over the chapters that include ways to save in your moving (such as mailing your books) and give serious thought to whether moving various items would be more expensive than replacing them.

● Keep careful track of all your moving expenses so you can justify them when you deduct them from your income tax return.

● Work out carefully the amount of money it will cost to move, and then add half as much again.

And if the total is more than you can face, start eliminating things and services.

Moving can prove one of the most stimulating experiences of life. It offers an opportunity to look at people, places, and ourselves in a different way.

Follow the suggestions in this book, and moving—whether around the corner, across the country, or halfway across the world—should be rewarding for you.

# Records to Keep for Internal Revenue Service

Air fare (to look for home)
Bus fare (to look for home)
Train fare (to look for home)
Automobile expenses (to look for home—so many
    miles at 7¢ a mile)
Meals (while looking for home)
Hotel or motel (while looking for home)
Advertising of old home
Appraisal charges
Commissions on real estate
Legal fees
Fees related to establishing title
State taxes
Cost of settling lease
Movers' packing and unpacking certificate (if any)
Certificate of weight of movers' van, loaded
Bill of Lading
Inventory
Air fare (to new home)
Bus fare (to new home)
Train fare (to new home)
Automobile expenses (to new home—so many miles
    at 7¢ a mile)
Meals (on way to new home)
Hotel or motel (on way to new home)
Meals (while waiting to move into new home)
Hotel or motel (while waiting to move into new
    home)

# GLOSSARY

Like all industries, the moving industry has its own terminology. This glossary is designed to define those terms you are most likely to encounter in the course of a move.

**agent**—The person or company in a city who acts for a moving company. Most of the largest (and best known) moving companies work through agents, and their performance can vary dramatically from one city to another depending on the particular agent.

**bill of lading**—The bill of lading is both a receipt for your household goods and a contract for its shipment. When you sign the bill of lading, you release your loaded household goods into the hands of the movers.

**certificate of packing and unpacking**—This shows the amount of packing and unpacking of your household goods that has been done by the movers at both ends of the move. In some cases, movers refuse to unpack even though this has been contracted for; make sure the certificate does not say it has been done.

**219**

**claim**—A statement by you about the loss or damage of any of your household goods during the course of the move. See Chapter 8, "Working with the Movers," for more information about making a claim. A claim is sent to the movers for settlement.

**declared valuation**—The amount you give as the value of your household goods. Take the highest valuation offered to ensure adequate coverage. The amount of the declared valuation is written in, by you, on the bill of lading.

**destination agent**—The individual or company at your new city who will supervise the delivery and unpacking (if any) of your household goods.

**driver**—The driver of the van that takes your household goods away is the top man on the movers' totem pole. The driver makes the inventory of your possessions and writes down what he considers their condition to be. If you disagree with his evaluation, make note of it. The driver may be called the "van operator."

**estimate**—Getting an estimate is the first step in making a move with professional movers. Get three estimates but, since an estimate is not a bid, don't be influenced by the lowest estimate. Look for a mover who seems at least moderately interested in moving your things; if the estimator gives you suggestions for ways to lower the total cost of the move, you have a real find. Regulations require that movers collect the total amount due before they unload your household goods at your new home—provided the total is no more than 110% of the estimate. If it is more, you must pay the 110% at once, but you have 15 working days to pay the balance.

**I.C.C. or Interstate Commerce Commission**—The federal agency that regulates movers. Complain to the I.C.C. if you run into trouble in the course of a move or if you are dissatisfied with the move later.

**inventory**—An inventory shows the number and gives a description of each of your household items. The inventory taken by the driver of a moving van also shows condition—as the driver sees it—of your household goods. Be sure you agree with his judgement and be sure you know what the letters used to describe condition mean.

**order for service**—You sign the order for service when you have selected the moving company (if any) that you will use.

**origin agent**—The individual or company that supervises the packing and loading of your household goods.

**performance report**—Every professional mover engaged in interstate commerce is required to give potential customers a copy of the company's performance report for the previous year. This provides such information as how many moves were over- or underestimated, how many moves were late, and so forth. Get the performance report when the estimator comes to look at your household goods—and complain if you don't.

**shipper**—You may hear yourself described as the shipper—it's used to describe the person who is sending household goods from one place to another.

**storage**—Keeping goods in the agent's warehouse.

**tariff**—In the sense used by moving companies, a listing of prices for various moving services. This is not handed out to customers—if you want to see the tariff of the moving company you plan to use, you will have to go to its offices and ask specifically. Since the charges on interstate moves are almost identical for all moving companies, there's no harm in skipping this.

**van operator**—The driver.

# INDEX